Praise for
Why Not You?

"If you're ready to stop playing small and start living up to your full potential, let Valorie lead you on this journey toward authentic confidence!"

—**Shannon Ethridge,** speaker and bestselling author of *Every Woman's Battle, Every Young Woman's Battle,* and nine other books

"Life coach Valorie Burton tells you how to find confidence."

—***Essence*** magazine

"*Why Not You?* is well written and full of practical suggestions, while undergirded with the caveat never to allow outside appearance to become more authentic than inner reality."

—**Mary Ann Mayo,** certified counselor and author of more than ten books, including *Twilight Travels with Mother,* on Alzheimer's

Praise for
Listen to Your Life
by Valorie Burton

"Unique...eloquent...conveying the intricacies of living life to the fullest.... Words of life to a hungry generation."

—**Bishop T. D. Jakes Sr.,** senior pastor of The Potter's House of Dallas Inc.

"Insightful words...personal touch. Burton teaches all to keep pushing, leading, and seeking the work we were placed on this earth to complete."

—**Dennis Kimbro,** author of *What Makes the Great Great*

"Inspiring, motivating, and packed with strategies that work…[moving] you to take action to transform your life."

—**Donna Richardson Joyner,** fitness expert, television host, and author of *Let's Get Real*

"The insight and revelation in this book will empower you to make better choices and to make your dreams become reality."

—**Les Brown,** motivational speaker and author of *Up Thoughts for Down Times* and *The Courage to Live Your Dreams*

"Captures the true essence of success, and its aroma is decisively God! Burton reveals the secret ingredients to a life well lived: passion, purpose, and destiny."

—**Andria Hall,** veteran broadcast journalist and author of *The Walk at Work: Seven Steps to Spiritual Success on the Job*

"The truths in this book will bring elements of beauty, strength, and honor to your life."

—**Lisa Bevere,** speaker and author of *Kissed the Girls and Made Them Cry*

"You won't be disappointed: dynamic introduction, distinctive format, reassuring conclusion; real-life applications, questions, and checklists that guide the process of successful living."

—**Connie Scott,** librarian, *Avid Reader Book Review*

Praise for

What's Really Holding You Back?

by Valorie Burton

"Answers that help you move into an abundant, fulfilling future."

—**Terry Meeuwsen,** co-host of *The 700 Club*

"The ticket to get you somewhere different from where you are. Burton saturates you with ultimate motivation and walks you through solutions that overcome every obstacle to your life's goals. Strategy has hit the mark."

—**Bishop Eddie L. Long,** senior pastor of New Birth Missionary Baptist Church and author of *Gladiator, Deliver Me From Adam, Wise Women,* and *Taking Over*

"With the skill of a surgeon, Burton dissects the major issues that hold us back, then provides the practical prescription for a breakthrough in each area. You will love this book!"

—**Bill Butterworth,** speaker and author of *The Promise of the Second Wind* and *New Life After Divorce*

"Just the boost you need. Inspiration that will take you to the next level."

—**Tom Joyner,** syndicated radio personality

"A solid, common-sense guide for folks with relationship, employment, weight, health, debt, career, faith, or other issues. Worthwhile for anyone stuck in a rut."

—**Kam Williams,** AALBC.com (African American Literature Book Clubs)

“Gives readers the insight, tools, and motivation needed to lead a healthier, wealthier, and wiser lifestyle.”

—**Edwin V. Avent,** publisher of *Heart and Soul* magazine

Praise for

Rich Minds, Rich Rewards

by Valorie Burton

“Lessons for living in fifty-two digestible chunks.”

—Library Journal

“A user-friendly, structured, year’s worth of once-a-week suggestions to achieve more success with less stress. A little workbook that goes a long way toward revitalizing your psyche.”

—Bookpage

28 Days to Authentic Confidence

Why Not You?

- Identify your Confidence Quotient
- Conquer doubt, hesitation, and insecurities
- Face the real source of your fears
- Eliminate your biggest confidence stealers

Valorie Burton

Author of **Listen to Your Life**

WATERBROOK
PRESS

WHY NOT YOU?
PUBLISHED BY WATERBROOK PRESS
12265 Oracle Boulevard, Suite 200
Colorado Springs, Colorado 80921
A division of Random House Inc.

Details in some anecdotes and stories have been changed to protect the identities of the persons involved.

ISBN 978-0-7394-8411-1

Printed in the United States of America

For my brother, Wade.
I believe in you.

Love, Val

Contents

An Introduction to Authentic Confidence

Why Not You?

Before I began writing books and speaking, I often studied authors and speakers who were doing what I wanted to do with my life. Their lives seemed somehow magical, as if they knew some special secrets that I didn't.

Of course, that wasn't true.

I had within me everything I needed to begin living the purpose for which I was created.

But what these other authors and speakers had that I didn't was confidence. Perseverance. That belief in yourself and your potential for success—so much so that you refuse to give up when success doesn't happen in your own timing.

I began asking myself, *Valorie, why not you? Why don't you fulfill your vision of inspiring others through your writing?*

Can you relate to that kind of internal questioning? Perhaps it's a similar area of life for you—a professional or business aspiration—or that conversation in your head may be about your weight, your dream of home ownership, your finances, or a successful relationship. Perhaps doubt or uncertainty results in your remaining quiet when you really want to speak up.

I had my moment of insight about the importance of boldly and confidently stepping into God-given opportunities, and it came within just a couple of years—back in 2001—after I began asking, *Why not me?*

Around five o'clock one Wednesday afternoon in October 2001, my phone rang as I was preparing to leave for a six-o'clock book signing at Black Images Books in Dallas. I lived in Dallas then; it was an exciting time. I was in the midst of a tour for my first book. *Rich Minds, Rich Rewards* had been self-published nearly two years earlier, but a major publisher had picked it up, and now their edition was on the shelves. I'd already been to Chicago, Detroit, and Los Angeles for interviews and book signings; now I was stopping back in Dallas for two days before heading out to Atlanta early the next morning.

When I answered my home-office line on the second ring, I recognized the voice on the other end immediately. "Hi, Valorie," said Rosilyn. We'd met six weeks earlier at the Texas Trailblazer Award luncheon, which I was chairing. Rosilyn was one of two representatives sent when Sister Serita Jakes, my pastor's wife—whom I'd invited to give the invocation—couldn't make the lunch because of her travels. I'd enjoyed Rosilyn, and we'd e-mailed back and forth a couple of times, promising to get together for lunch sometime. We hadn't managed to put a date on our calendars yet, so I thought this may be why she was calling.

It wasn't.

"Listen," she said. "Bishop Jakes is launching a new daily television show."

"Oh, yes, I've heard about that," I replied. "That's really exciting." Trying to contain my own excitement, I wondered, *Is she going to ask if I want to be a guest on the show!?* My first book had just been released, and I was overjoyed at the idea of being on Bishop Jakes's television show. I'd been up late one night when, during a broadcast, I heard Paul Crouch, founder of Trinity Broadcasting Network, offer a yearlong timeslot to Bishop Jakes if he would provide a daily show for the viewers. Mind you, Rosilyn was still in midsentence, and already my mind had launched ahead to figuring out the reason for her call. Of course, if I would just be patient and listen, I'd find out soon enough.

"We haven't yet found a co-host for the program," she continued.

Maybe she wants me to recommend somebody? I thought before she had a chance to finish.

"I know you're not a television person…," she said, almost apologetically.

No, she can't be asking if I want to co-host a national television show?

"But we're here in the studio, and I prayed about it, and your name is the only name God dropped in my spirit."

Did she just ask me…, I started to wonder.

"Would you be willing to serve as our co-host for the first few weeks while we figure out what direction to take?" Rosilyn finally asked.

"Wow. Um, yes," I said. "I would love to." I was excited and in a state of disbelief. After all, it isn't every day that someone calls you out of the blue to ask you to host a national television program with someone you greatly admire and respect. *Is this really happening?*

She explained that I would need to come to the studio right away or at least by the next day and that I should bring an assortment of clothes.

Oh no, I thought, and then I had to explain that I was already on the way to a book signing that would start in an hour and that I was scheduled to leave before sunrise the next morning for a flight to Atlanta. I wouldn't be back until the weekend!

But maybe…

I suggested, due to their schedule and my book tour, the only option was for me to rush over after my book signing.

"Could you?" Rosilyn asked.

That's exactly what I kept asking myself as I packed my clothes and headed off for a whirlwind evening. *Can I do this?* I wondered as I finished the book signing at Black Images downtown and headed to the studio about twenty-five miles north.

It was going on nine o'clock, and when I arrived, there were about ten people there—producers, camera people, and ministry staff. They explained what was needed, a few ins and outs for five days worth of programming, and just one catch.

There was no script, and I wouldn't be able to see the show I'd be referring to on-camera.

Oh.

I took a deep, quiet breath for composure. I was unsure, but there was no need to show it.

They sat me in a chair, aimed a camera at me, and "Three…two…one," the director said as his fingers counted down. On "zero," he pointed at me.

I prayed and then felt a sense of confidence rise within me. I'd spent the previous three months being interviewed weekly on KXAS-TV (NBC5) in Dallas, so I'd begun to get used to talking into a camera. I decided that experience must have been God's preparation.

To calm my nervousness, I did a reality check and took stock of the situation. I knew if I thought of this as a big deal—a show that would be seen daily around the country and in multiple foreign countries—I'd get nervous. So I told myself, "You're just talking to some people while they start their day by enjoying great biblical teaching from T. D. Jakes." I reminded myself that television is experienced one person at a time. By thinking in these terms, I was able to find a peaceful place from which to speak.

I've since pursued my passion of inspiring others to live fulfilling lives, and along the way, I've gained tremendous confidence in God's ability to carry out His purposes through each one of us. It's our confidence in Him that bolsters our confidence and belief in ourselves. Knowing that God created you and wants to use you also means acknowledging that He accepts you as you are. Simultaneously, He's offering you daily opportunities to grow into more of the person He created you to be. He accepts you, despite the criticisms, doubts, or insecurities you may impose on yourself and the obstacles you erect for yourself.

So why is the issue of overcoming doubt and building confidence one of the most important for you to address?

Maybe because it impacts your:

- relationships, as in whether you stand up for yourself, set good boundaries, and choose mutually beneficial friendships
- finances, since insecurity and self-doubt are leading contributors to overwhelming credit-card debt as people attempt to fill a void through overspending
- ability to parent your children effectively
- chosen career (or the career you don't choose), including how quickly you advance and how much money you earn

In fact, to see the depth of the effects of lacking confidence, take this little self-quiz: Which of the following statements would you like to be able to say are true about you? Check the statements that are true for you now, and give yourself one point for each.

- ☐ I can walk into a room full of strangers and introduce myself, be friendly, and feel comfortable.

- □ I can successfully make a presentation in front of a group of people.
- □ Fear doesn't stop me from asking for what I want.
- □ If I purchase something that proves faulty, I can return it to the store that has an unfriendly refund policy and ask for—and receive—a refund.
- □ I don't have to chase after success. Because I work hard and live my purpose, the right opportunities, people, and resources find their way to my path.
- □ I always trust myself to finish what I start.
- □ If I make a mistake, I never try to cover it up or explain it away with excuses in order to look good. I'm comfortable with being imperfect.
- □ I have (or am moving toward) exactly what I want in my life. I haven't settled in any way.
- □ I'm financially confident and have proven myself to be a good steward of money.
- □ I can walk into a dinner party and feel confident about how I look. I don't size up other attendees and compare my looks, clothes, jewelry, or other characteristics with theirs.

If you're like most people, you weren't able to truthfully check all ten statements, because doubts, fears, and insecurities creep into our lives in ways we often don't even notice, let alone identify as a confidence issue.

I have written *Why Not You?* as a personal companion to help you confront these things and build your confidence over a twenty-eight-day period—a progressive plan to maintain or increase your confidence, boldness, and self-esteem throughout your life in order to live fully and freely, to realize your potential, and to be faithful to God's will for you.

Confidence is essential because it's a tool that empowers you to do everything God created you to do. With confidence, you never have to look back on life with regret wondering what you "coulda, shoulda, woulda" done...if only you'd had the confidence.

Strengthening your confidence empowers you to say yes to God consistently and without hesitation.

In an effort to gain confidence, thousands of people undergo surgery every year to change their looks. They hope that if they're more attractive, they'll finally feel secure and confident enough to pursue the life they really want. There's no doubt that cosmetic or material improvements may help people feel better, and surface results can be obtained quickly. Just drive a more expensive-looking car and notice how certain people treat you differently. Slip on an expensive piece of jewelry before you go shopping and notice how much more attentively you're treated by some of the salespeople in stores.

Yes, there are quick remedies to calm our insecurities and doubts. But if the change is only physical, authentic confidence will never emerge, and the glimmers will never last. Purely surface changes attract surface results.

Is that all *you* really want?

What I want you to know is that who you are right now is enough.

In fact, it's more than enough for you to walk, speak, and live confidently in every situation you face in life. You don't need to be more attractive, more talented, more connected, wealthier, or anything else to be confident.

You are enough because God is enough.

As you turn the pages of this book and go deeper in trusting God's perfect plan for you, I challenge you to notice how you'll lose your desire to be around people whose interest in you is based on what you have, how you look, and what you can do. You'll naturally begin attracting relationships based on who you are—your purpose, inherent value, and divinely created uniqueness.

Are you ready to move to a new level of living in some area of your life? Are you ready to stop holding your tongue, shrinking from opportunities, and allowing pesky insecurities to sabotage your relationships, finances, or career? Are you ready to deal with the doubts about your abilities and your dreams that creep in from time to time?

We've all stood in awe of those we view as successful, believing they have something we don't have and—worse yet—something we may never get. The truth is, we'll never really be successful doing anything other than the things each of us were uniquely and specially created to do.

The time has come for you to make a major change—a change that empowers you to believe fully and confidently in yourself. Now is the time for you to break out of any self-imposed limitation and allow the real you to fully emerge.

I know that nothing but good can come from doing so. And here's one reason I know. I stumbled onto the need for this topic in 2005 when respondents to a questionnaire in my weekly e-newsletter, *Rich Minds, Rich Rewards,* said that what held them back most in life were insecurity, doubt, and lack of confidence.

I had simply been asking questions to discover the personal growth topics of greatest interest to my readers, and about fifteen hundred people from across the United States and in many other countries responded. I asked about twenty questions, most of them multiple choice, with a couple open-ended questions too, such as, "What's the biggest obstacle to achieving your vision?" And, I admit, I expected the most common responses to be fear, money, or lack of knowledge.

To my surprise, the most common answer was some variation of these responses:

- Karen, 36, in Sunrise, Florida, said, "I can't seem to overcome the persistent feeling that I'm not good enough. I wonder if I'm intelligent enough and if people will take me seriously."
- Tammy, 34, from Illinois, said, "I don't have enough self-confidence to pursue my dreams. I'm not sure how much potential I have."
- Alex, 37, from Holland said, "My biggest obstacle is self-confidence —or lack thereof."
- Karen, 51, in Fargo, North Dakota, said, "I know my vision. I'm just missing the confidence and know-how to do it."

Confidence. Self-esteem. These two engines that take us places are, more often than not, missing. Why is that?

It's one of the first lessons we're all taught, and yet so quickly forget later when we're finally able to step into our dreams and goals.

Do you remember, when we were children, hearing such things as, "If you just put your mind to it, you can do anything"?

It may have been a schoolteacher who said this or a parent, relative, or actor speaking on some children's television show.

I remember the intrigue I felt the first time I heard the story of the little engine that could, who made it up the hill repeating the mantra, *"I think I can, I think I can, I think I can…"*

Did the engine really make it because he thought he could? I remember asking myself.

Even then, though I didn't understand why thinking he could do something enabled him to do it, I chose to believe that this approach would work!

Adults are quick to encourage children about what's possible in life.

That's a good thing. In fact, it's biblical. "As he thinks in his heart, so is he," reads Proverbs 23:7 (NKJV).

But I think children assume that adults believe their own rhetoric. Too often, we don't. The disappointments and negative experiences of life can steal your confidence if you allow them to, jading your attitude and diminishing your sense of optimism.

Building authentic confidence is an essential element of personal growth. You can know what to do, how to do it, who can help you, and where to go, but if you lack confidence that you can accomplish certain things in your life, none of that knowledge will matter.

I'm afraid that too many people hear Scripture, and even repeat it, but don't believe God's Word for themselves:

- "With God all things are possible" (Matthew 19:26).
- "I can do all things through Christ who strengthens me" (Philippians 4:13, NKJV).
- "As he thinks in his heart, so is he" (Proverbs 23:7, NKJV).

The Scriptures are not just sayings to be memorized. They're truths filled with wisdom by which to live our lives.

You are fully equipped to do and be all that you were meant to. Even those who have confidence by the world's standards often lack authentic confidence—that is, confidence by God's standards. Authentic confidence is self-confidence built on a foundation of faith. It's a clear understanding that your abilities, when teamed with God's power and will, are unstoppable.

And yet authentic confidence gets beaten out of people. I discovered that while researching this book. I created an informal confidence survey and questioned more than three hundred people. The respondents had diverse backgrounds, but many experienced very similar challenges around the issue of confidence. You will see comments from these respondents throughout the book. My hope is that you will see some aspects of yourself in their triumphs and struggles. You're not alone on this path. Here are some basic facts about the survey respondents I'll refer to from time to time throughout the book:

- Age: 24 percent are twenty-five to thirty-four years old; 45 percent are thirty-five to forty-four years old; and 22 percent are forty-five to fifty-four years old.
- Highest educational level attained: 35 percent have some college education, vocational training, or an associate's degree; 32 percent have earned a bachelor's degree; 20 percent have earned a master's degree; and 4 percent have earned a terminal degree (doctorate, law degree, medical doctorate).
- Gender: 94 percent of respondents were women.
- Residence: 98 percent reside in the United States and the remainder, in Canada and Europe. Respondents from the United States hail from forty states and the District of Columbia.
- Career: Their careers include entrepreneur, attorney, administrative assistant, engineer, retail manager, teacher, nurse, college professor, sales executive, cake decorator, journalist, and stay-at-home mom.

I've written this book so that you might internalize and manifest the truth of God's Word in your life by living confidently every day. What does it look like for a person to know the Scriptures yet not truly believe them? He or she—or you—might do one of the following:

- shrink from opportunities out of fear you are not good enough, smart enough, attractive enough, and so forth
- put others on a pedestal
- buy or seek material possessions in an effort to prove or display your worth

- try to stack up credentials in an effort to achieve things God has uniquely prepared you to do
- not stand up for yourself
- allow negative experiences from your past to steal your confidence
- display arrogance about abilities and/or achievements
- lack humility
- buy in to the notion that you've achieved success because you're "better" than others
- regularly measure your value by comparing yourself with others, whether professionally or personally
- have more confidence in yourself than you have in God's ability to orchestrate situations to your advantage

Both arrogance and timidity stem from a lack of knowledge and wisdom about God's Word, His promises, and His character. Arrogance and timidity are manifestations of insecurity, self-doubt, and fear that lead to a lack of authentic confidence.

In *Why Not You?* we'll explore the basic pillars for authentic self-confidence as well as shifts and changes you can make beginning today to become a more faith-filled, confident person over the next twenty-eight days.

I encourage you to read this book with a partner or group, so that you may talk out the issues discussed and hold one another accountable as you take steps forward in faith. If you choose to read it alone, that's fine! Don't allow not having a partner or group to be an obstacle. I offer actions and confidence-building exercises that can be done in a group or individually.

In this book, I open my own life to you and share many personal examples as well as stories from the lives of people like you. From every example are drawn practical, spiritual lessons.

What I want for you is to be so sure of yourself, so confident in your potential, that you experience all that God has in store for you. I don't want you to shrink any longer from who you really are in order to make others happy or to stay inside your comfort zone. When opportunity knocks, I want you to be ready to answer and fully confident about doing so.

I've experienced the pain of allowing doubt to overwhelm me in a moment of opportunity. I've also learned to step up to the plate—despite the persistence of doubts that crossed my mind.

"Be prepared in season and out of season," the apostle Paul advised Timothy (2 Timothy 4:2). Authentic confidence will empower you to be ready to serve God in any situation.

Remember my moment of empowerment in front of the television cameras? Isn't it amazing the way God can supernaturally infuse you with confidence if you ask Him to? And remember Jesus's promise: "Ask and it will be given to you; seek and you will find; knock and the door will be opened to you" (Matthew 7:7).

We never know the ways in which a lack of confidence usurps our success because often multiple opportunities are born out of one simple connection. So it's essential to your personal and professional success to be ready and confident when opportunities cross your path. Many times you simply won't have time to research and prepare. You'll need to stand on what you already know and do your best with what you have in that moment. Authentic confidence will empower you with that skill.

For nearly a year in 2001 and 2002, I served on the air as the co-host of *The Potter's Touch,* and I also helped create show ideas and coordinate guests. It was an awesome and divinely orchestrated opportunity. I grew and learned a lot quickly.

In addition to the terrific broadcasting experience it gave me, the television program also opened doors for me to meet two wonderful friends. One of them is like a sister to me, and the other connected me with the person who introduced me to an editor of my current publisher. Had I not had the confidence to rise to the occasion when the opportunity presented itself, these doors might not have opened.

Why Not You? is a twenty-eight-day program written in twenty-eight small chapters so that you may digest the information and take action daily over the next four weeks.

At the end of each chapter are three important tools for you to use to connect more deeply with yourself and God—and to stretch yourself so that God can shape you into a more confident person:

- *Confidence Prayer:* A simple way for you to direct your thoughts to God and ask Him for the strength and wisdom you need in the particular area addressed in that chapter.
- *Confidence Journal:* This is the assignment part, but you don't have to be a writer. Journal if you choose, or just make notes in response to the simple question or series of questions designed to empower you to unearth your potential by addressing the issues, challenges, and possibilities that lie ahead of you. I recommend you get a special journal or notebook in which to write your answers and thoughts.
- *Confidence Builder:* This is the all-important action step—and this book isn't meant to be read passively. It will only work if you step out in faith and take action toward becoming a more confident person who daily conquers doubt, hesitation, and fear to enjoy success in every area of life.

Don't skip over these three tools! If you use them over the next twenty-eight days, you'll transform your level of confidence and significantly enhance your quality of life.

Throughout this book, you'll also notice that the topics addressed can be categorized in four ways:

1. *Truth.* It's important to see the reality of where you are. What are the issues you need to address? What aspects of your past hold clues to the doubts or insecurities that are most persistent in your mind? Are you stuck in a rut of overachieving in order to compensate for other areas? As your coach, I'll help you get a grip on your truth as a starting point for building authentic confidence.
2. *Faith.* Since authentic confidence is based on faith in God's will and plan for you, absolutely key is your spiritual foundation as a cornerstone. We'll talk about how to conquer doubt, just be yourself, put a stop to competing and comparing yourself with others, unravel cultural lies, manage emotional behaviors that sabotage your success, and discover the power of body language to make you feel more confident.
3. *Preparation.* Authentic confidence will enable you to take steps toward realizing your potential, and that means not waiting for God to hand you your desired circumstances on a silver platter. Rather, it's about maximizing what God has already blessed you with and preparing for the opportunities that will ultimately come, so that when it's time for you to perform, you've no reason to lack confidence. My aim is to encourage you to prepare intentionally so that you'll be ready for opportunities when they do cross your path.
4. *Transformation:* Last, I'll encourage you to strengthen your courage and faith so that you can transform your behavior with new actions that reflect your authentic confidence. You'll learn the powerful influence of humility, how to set healthy boundaries, how to overcome the temptation to lapse into old habits, how to develop the effective technique of "cross-confidence," and how to be confident even when you do not feel confident.

Thank you for allowing me the privilege of serving as your coach and friend on your journey to authentic confidence. It will be an experience of self-discovery and becoming more of who God intends you to be!

Ready?

Let's get started.

Day 1

Take Stock of Yourself

> What kind of confidence does it take to truly succeed? People like Oprah, Donald Trump, U.S. presidents, company CEOs, pastors of megachurches—what kind of confidence do they have? What do they have that I don't? Are they smarter? less fearful? crazy?
>
> —Alison, 34

When I finished graduate school, what I really wanted to do was to be a reporter or perhaps a news anchor. That was my dream job at the time, and I'd worked hard to earn a master's in journalism with an emphasis in broadcasting. I prepared educationally, and then it was time to step into the field.

Did I go for it?

Nope. I hate to admit it, but the truth is I never even tried. Paralyzed by my fear that I hadn't learned enough and didn't have what it takes, I didn't send out a single tape to a newsroom. Persistent doubts kept me from pursuing my dream.

Instead, I pursued a career that seemed more attainable to me at the time—public relations. I'd be able to use my journalism skills and would interact with the media, but I denied myself the joy of going for my dream at a time in life when I truly had nothing to lose.

I refer to this phenomenon as downsizing your dream. Even as I write these words, I can still feel the sorrow that comes with burying a dream because I allowed doubt and a lack of confidence to steer me onto a less challenging path.

For several years, I never told anyone the truth about why I'd chosen public relations, and I've since learned three tremendous lessons:

1. Life is too short to allow doubt to keep you from doing the things you really want to do.
2. A little talent and a healthy dose of authentic confidence based on living your unique purpose will always lead to success.
3. The phrase "I'm not good enough" isn't worthy of my use.

These lessons are true for you as well. If the dream involves something God created you to do, you'll always be good enough to do it. But that doesn't mean the steps there will be easy. You see, building confidence means engaging in spiritual warfare. It also means you can expect doubt when you step outside your comfort zone. "Put on the full armor of God, so that when the day of evil comes, you may be able to stand your ground, and after you have done everything, to stand," Ephesians 6:13 advises. The enemy wants you to remain bound and stagnant. So he persistently and relentlessly places seeds of doubt in your mind to keep you from moving closer to God's plan for your life.

Confidence, ultimately, is about trust. When you take the focus off of attempting to control things yourself and trust God's ability to orchestrate your life, you understand on the deepest level that, with God, all things are possible.

In light of that truth, why do we battle a lack of confidence so much?

I believe it's because we're in a constant spiritual battle—a battle for our minds—and the primary weapon used against us is doubt. Doubt is a mighty and forceful weapon against those who do not clothe themselves in the armor of truth that is God's Word. Doubt, as you've probably experienced (I know I have!), is persistent and relentless. It steals your confidence and your dreams. It causes you to shrink from who you are.

Have you ever wanted to do something but stopped yourself because you thought, *I'm not good enough? I'm not attractive enough? I'm not talented enough? My educational background isn't good enough? I'm not financially successful enough?*

The "not enough" syndrome shuts down many dreams and desires. Rather than confidently pursuing our dreams and goals despite our doubts, we censor ourselves as protection from the possibility that our doubts might prove true. Believing that you're not enough will create a fear that paralyzes you and keeps you from building fully on what you *do* have enough of. What dream are you burying right now because of persistent doubts or a lack of confidence that you can bring your dream to life?

Our culture too often encourages us to place our confidence in things that have no power to give us *authentic* confidence—in material possessions, looks, talents, money, and people, just to name a few. If we must look a certain way to be confident, then inevitably a large percentage of the population will never have confidence. And even those who have the right look won't maintain that look forever. So, at some point, even they will lose their supposed confidence. Have you ever felt great about how you looked only to have someone else show up looking better than you did? In those moments did your insecurity rise and confidence wane?

Perhaps it isn't looks for you, but instead you've based your confidence on material possessions. When you wear the right brand, don expensive jewelry, drive an impressive car, or live in a prestigious neighborhood or home, you feel confident. But without those things, you feel lost or unimportant. You may aspire to those things right now because you believe they'll give you the confidence, security, and self-esteem you long for.

Or maybe it isn't looks or material possessions that do it for you. Instead, you base your confidence on how well you perform. When your career or business is doing well, your income increases or you make the dean's list, your confidence soars. You thrive on your knowledge and performance. When you feel good about what you do, you are confident. But what happens when you enter an area in which you don't know how to perform well? Perhaps you avoid those areas altogether. You have little confidence in your ability to maintain a relationship, for instance, so you put all your energy into your work because that's something you do well.

The problem with basing our confidence on what we do, what we have, how we look, and who we know is that those things are circumstantial. Authentic confidence is based on principles that are powerful, permanent, and immediately accessible. In this moment, you are good enough, talented enough, and attractive enough to accomplish all that God has set before you.

I invite you to make a shift right now in your thinking. It's a shift that empowers you to embrace the perfection in who you are and to trust that everything you need to succeed is within you right now. When I say "perfection in who you are," I'm not suggesting that you're perfect. None of us is perfect, but each of us was uniquely created by God—and He made no mistakes when He created you. I bet you could thumb through your mental Rolodex of personal imperfections you'd like to see changed. Even those imperfections, however, are perfect because as you persevere through them, God uses the opportunities to further develop you into the person He created you to be.

So there's perfection in your imperfections. They are teaching tools for your personal growth and development. In that, you can be confident.

In order to embody authentic confidence, you must trust that God has uniquely created you for a purpose. All that makes you who you are is purposeful. You must trust that you have value beyond your own comprehension, value that's divinely connected to the world around you. Confidence isn't so much about you as it is about God working through you.

The purpose of this book is to build your confidence by building your faith—and faith requires you to face reality, God's reality.

Reality has become more difficult for the faith-filled person to discern than ever before. "Reality" television suggests that outrageous, flashy, rude, crass, selfish, and self-centered behavior is real—and that the rest of us are out of touch.

The true reality is that love and service are the real reasons for being. There is no higher calling than spending your time and energy on loving and serving. If you follow this path, anchored in God's truth, you can know beyond a shadow of a doubt that you need nothing more to succeed in God's eyes.

Trust Him.

Believe Him.

Have faith in His ways.

Nothing else in life matters more than knowing we are successful according to God's standards. There is no greater foundation for confidence.

Confidence Prayer

Thank You for creating me just as You did, Lord. I trust that even my imperfections are perfect tools for You to use to grow me into the person I am meant to be. Empower me to be fully confident in who I am and where I am at this stage in my life. Open my eyes to the reality that I am good enough, talented enough, and attractive enough to live out every purpose for which I am here on this earth right now. When seeds of doubt tempt me to downsize the dreams You place in my heart, give me the strength to resist them. On this journey toward confidence, help me always anchor myself in the truth and reality of Your ways. Help me trust, believe, and have faith.

Confidence Journal

In what ways do you want to be different at the completion of this twenty-eight-day journey toward authentic confidence? Write down some specific traits. If certain situations give rise to the traits you'd like to change, describe what happens and how you feel before and after.

Confidence Builder

Today, face reality. It is essential to counter doubt with the truth. Identify one way in which you feel that you are not enough—not talented, good, attractive, or smart enough. Now make a "Truth" list stating all the reasons you *are* enough.

Day 2

Know that Authentic Confidence Attracts Success

> My confidence emerges from my sense of knowing I'm doing the right thing, the thing I feel God has called me to do.
>
> —Catherine, 36

Authentic confidence is more than self-confidence. Self-confidence is about what *you* can do. Authentic confidence is about what *God* can do through you, in you, and for you.

It's important to possess self-confidence, build your skills, properly prepare to fulfill your dreams, and learn through experience and education. But these things aren't enough; they'll never be enough. It takes a force much larger than you to realize your greatest potential. When you recognize that this force—God—is with you wherever you go, guiding and directing you, using you, protecting you, and teaching you, you suddenly have an edge. Trust that for those who love God and live according to His purpose for their lives, *all things work together for good* (see Romans 8:28).

If all things are working together for your good, you have every reason to be confident. Even when you mess up, circumstances will eventually work together for your good. Think back to a situation in your life in which you lacked confidence and fear gripped you. You made it through, didn't you? Maybe you didn't get the outcome you were looking for at that time, but the experience taught you something. The experience moved you in a new direction and expanded you in some way.

Knowing that God is with you is a key to authentic confidence. So authentic confidence is self-confidence *plus* faith. Authentic confidence is your complete trust that what you offer to this world is valuable, meaningful, and divinely unique. Self-confidence is an important element of authentic confidence, but it does not replace or supersede authentic confidence.

Authentic confidence acknowledges that your life is bigger than you. Authentic confidence is having faith that all things will work together for your good when you follow the path of your purpose and act in ways that demonstrate your love for God (see Romans 8:28). The question you must settle for yourself is, *What am I basing my confidence on?*

Authentic confidence gives you the ability to be secure in who you are, in your right to be yourself in every situation, and in the certainty that God can use you despite your imperfections. To exude confidence, you don't need to grasp something outside of yourself. You don't need to look a certain way, possess certain skills, or have a certain amount of money in your bank account. Who you are is enough.

As talented as the world's best-known talents are, I'm convinced there are many more people, just as gifted, who pass through this world without ever fully sharing their talent.

Why?

Because talent, without the confidence to share it fully, goes undeveloped and unappreciated.

Countless relationships suffer because people refuse to muster the confidence to stand up for themselves or for what they know is best. If they did, the entire dynamic of these relationships would shift. It takes confidence to become all that God created you to be. It takes confidence to say, "I know my purpose, and I'm going to live it every day." In our politically correct world, it takes confidence to say unashamedly, "I believe in Jesus Christ, and my daily goal is to follow His example."

More than ever before, believers must be bold and confident. It takes confidence to believe you can bring children into this world and raise them to be productive, positive, and successful members of society. There are days when you simply will not feel like you have the ability to do it even though you do.

It takes confidence to handle difficult people and tough situations with ease. You might have the talent and skills to do it, but the more important question is, "Do you believe in your ability?" Ultimately, talent will only take you so far. You have to believe in yourself, and more important, you have to believe that God is with you and has a vested interest in your success.

Somewhere along the journey, many of you have picked up the idea that in order to be confident, you have to know the answers. You have to be the most talented, most educated, or most skilled. But confidence is derived, in large part, from believing that the knowledge about how to achieve a goal is within your reach. Authentic confidence is comfortable with a lack of information right now because you know that you can find the information. "I don't know how to do that" is simply not an obstacle for you when you are authentically confident. "I'll find out how" is your steppingstone. This type of attitude attracts success. It's an attitude of trust and an attitude that believes God will light your path—an attitude that acknowledges that your path may be unconventional. And you know what? That's okay.

Let me tell you about one such unconventional path. René Syler is the former co-host of *The Early Show* weekday mornings on CBS. I first met her in 1998 when she was a news anchor in Dallas and a nominee for the Texas Trailblazer Award luncheon, an event I chaired at the time. After the event that day, my father and I sat outside the ballroom of the Anatole Hotel and talked with René. I was intrigued by the path she'd taken to get into television. She clearly had the talent for television, but she didn't have the education or skills when she decided to enter the industry.

I interviewed René for my column on BlackAmericaWeb.com, and I want to share her story with you here. Notice how she confidently set out to learn the skills and make the sacrifices necessary to reach her goal. It takes authentic confidence to say, "I don't know how to do this right now, but I'll create a path to learn and get my foot in the door." And notice that her being confident doesn't mean never feeling insecurity or fear.

> René Syler's success is proof that giving yourself the freedom to change paths can sometimes be the best career move of all. "I was in graduate school studying psychology, but it simply wasn't feeding my soul," René told me. "I had to find something that was a better fit for me."
>
> She found that fit in television news. Millions enjoy her warm, positive style and one-on-one interviews with entertainers, authors, and political newsmakers such as First Lady Laura Bush, [former] Secretary of State Colin Powell, and Senator John McCain. The idea for her career was sparked by a newspaper article that crossed Syler's

path in 1986. It was about a Boston newscaster named Liz Walker, who at the time, was the highest paid African American woman in television news. Syler had an insatiable appetite for news and information—and the article triggered an epiphany that changed the course of her career: drop out of graduate school and pursue a career in broadcast journalism.

"When you discover your passion, you've got to go for it," she said. "You can't wait for an opportunity. You have to make the opportunity."

And that's just what she did. With a bachelor's degree in psychology and a handful of graduate courses, both from California State University at Sacramento, she refused to beat herself up for not choosing the right major earlier. Instead, she left graduate school and enrolled in a community college, where she took journalism classes to learn the basics. She landed a six-month internship at the Fox affiliate in her hometown of Sacramento, California, where she learned production on the clock and spent her off-hours hanging out in the newsroom with reporters and anchors.

"I took a backdoor approach. I learned production first," she said.

As soon as she had a demo tape in hand from her work as an intern, Syler called a news director in nearby Reno and asked if she could drop off a tape because she was "going to be in town." She didn't bother to mention that the only reason she was coming to town was to meet him. Her boldness paid off, and in 1987 KTVN-TV in Reno offered her a job as a reporter. Just one little catch: she'd have to survive on a salary of $15,000 per year.

"I was on television. I had to have clothes, and you know hair is a huge expense for black women," Syler recalled. "I made $474 every two weeks, and I had to make it last. So I kept a bag of potatoes in my desk drawer at work. Every day at lunch, I'd have a potato with some hot sauce on it. That's what I had to do to get started."

After two years at her first station, Syler moved on to another station in Reno, then on to Birmingham. By 1992, she was the morning and noon anchor in a top 10 market, at Dallas's ABC affiliate WFAA-TV. In 1997, she became an anchor at Dallas's KTVT-TV, a station owned by CBS. Network executives were impressed with Syler and tapped her for *The Early Show* in October 2002, making her the first African American woman to co-host a network morning show.

Like many professionals, Syler says that she still struggles with fear and insecurity at times. "I prepare as much as possible every day, but I always feel like I can do even better. With millions watching, it can be easy to second-guess your performance."

We too often look at others whom we deem successful and confident and believe that somehow they knew it all when they started. It simply isn't true. Those people we place on a pedestal of success often aren't more equipped, but they are bolder in their belief in themselves. They understand and are comfortable with not personally knowing all the answers. They get to the core of information that is needed and build from there.

In what areas of your life are you shrinking from your possibilities because of a lack of skills, education, or know-how?

____

____

What step could you take toward embracing your possibilities despite this perceived lack?

____

____

____

You'll attract success when you begin thinking you can achieve success. Others will begin to have greater confidence in you, which in turn will build your confidence in yourself. This resolve that says, "I'll figure out how to do it," causes others to trust you—and, even more important, causes you to trust yourself. When people know you can be trusted to handle a situation, they are less concerned with what you know than with the fact that you will not become flustered, give up easily, or get rattled. You can be trusted to handle whatever comes your way.

So I challenge you to let go of the idea that your talent and know-how are the only key elements of personal or professional success. An abundance of confidence will take you further than talent or know-how. And two essentials of confidence are faith and trust in God—trust that He will make available to you the resources you need—and your ability to communicate effectively. It's this combination of faith and communication that lead to success.

Later in this book, we will discuss ways for you to communicate with confidence. While talent, skills, know-how, and education are indeed important to success, they're often secondary to confidence—but you need both. Authentic confidence (self-confidence plus faith) will get your foot in the door, but your skills will keep you there. No amount of confidence will make up for a lack of substance.

For sustained success—whether at work or in your personal life—one is not much good without the other. Authentic confidence can compensate for a lack of talent, and abundant talent can compensate for a small lack of confidence. Most often, however, I've observed that a solid level of authentic confidence combined with a solid amount of talent can produce consistently stellar results. Think for a moment about exceptional people—exceptional in terms of skills, appearance, or education—who did not find the most success, but instead success went to the person who stepped out in faith and communicated effectively. Authentic confidence attracts success. A lack of confidence and arrogance (false confidence) repel it.

So I challenge you to focus as much on embracing authentic confidence as you do on developing your skills, education, and talent. This principle applies at work as well as in your relationships, in your finances as well as in your health.

Notice in this chart a few of the ways that confidence and talent intertwine in the five key areas of your life. Talent and education are important to achieving success, but authentic confidence is the foundation that attracts and sustains success.

Talent and education alone are not enough to maximize your potential. You need authentic confidence to empower you to realize your full potential. I encourage you to hone your skills and sharpen your experience and education. Then believe in God's ability to open doors and increase opportunities for you.

	AUTHENTIC CONFIDENCE	TALENT, SKILLS, EDUCATION
SPIRITUAL LIFE	▪ surrendering control to God ▪ fully trusting Him ▪ being obedient to His Word because you believe His promises ▪ living your purpose	▪ memorizing Scripture ▪ going to church ▪ reading the Bible ▪ praying

	AUTHENTIC CONFIDENCE	TALENT, SKILLS, EDUCATION
WORK LIFE	▪ being willing to take divinely inspired risks ▪ believing in yourself ▪ following your passion ▪ stepping up to the plate for assignments and opportunities that take you outside your comfort zone	▪ completing a formal education ▪ gaining on-the-job experience ▪ developing sheer technical talent ▪ training
FINANCIAL LIFE	▪ trusting God and following divinely guided financial plans ▪ not trying to "keep up with the Joneses" because you are confident and content with where you are right now ▪ asking for a raise ▪ negotiating compensation for your services that values your worth ▪ investing your money after studying your options	▪ sharpening business skills ▪ developing entrepreneurial know-how ▪ managing money wisely ▪ understanding the importance of saving ▪ knowing the dangers of debt
HEALTH	▪ taking action toward good health daily ▪ taking extremely good care of yourself because it glorifies God and you deserve it ▪ trusting that you can develop the discipline you need ▪ going to the doctor when something isn't right	▪ knowing and choosing a balanced diet ▪ exercising regularly and effectively
RELATIONSHIPS	▪ not settling for less kindness and respect than you deserve ▪ being authentic and truthful in your interactions ▪ building meaningful connections with others ▪ standing up for yourself ▪ saying what needs to be said ▪ giving and receiving respect	▪ learning from raising your first child so that it's easier with the second and third ▪ knowing how to network effectively ▪ developing better relationship skills through books, counseling, coaching, mentoring, seminars

"Seek first his kingdom and his righteousness, and all these things will be given to you as well," Matthew 6:33 promises. Focus on serving God, doing good, and being excellent. He'll do the rest.

"For whoever finds me finds life and receives favor from the LORD," Proverbs 8:35 says. God can open doors you never even knew existed—and those doors are not necessarily dependent on your talent, skills, and education. If it's what God has in store for you, His divine favor will be enough.

Two preachers whose messages continually impact my life are Joyce Meyer and Joel Osteen. The anointing of God is obvious in their ministries. Despite having some of the largest congregations and conferences in the United States, neither of these ministers graduated from divinity school or college. Their life experience, incredible ability to connect with people and minister to real needs, and their personal study of God's Word are among the most important credentials God has used to expand their ministries. These people remind me that God doesn't always call the qualified, but He always qualifies those He calls.

Confidence Prayer

Lord, today I surrender control of my life to You. I choose to trust that if I follow Your will for my life, I cannot fail. In that, I can have full confidence. Help me fully acknowledge and sharpen the skills You have given me. Guide me to use them fully in every area of my life. Grant me the authentic confidence to let go of fear and step out in faith to accomplish all that You have set before me.

Confidence Journal

What gifts, talents, or skills are currently going unused or underutilized in your life? If you've already tapped into certain gifts, talents, or skills, what impact has that had on your life? What are you busy trying to "qualify" yourself to do? Is God leading you to gain more education or qualifications—or is your fear that you're not good enough and your sense that you need more credentials stopping you from stepping out in faith?

Confidence Builder

Revisit the chart in this chapter about how authentic confidence intertwines with talent and education. Then identify a skill about which you lack confidence. Make a decision to trust God to compensate for your perceived lack—either through His favor or through His guiding you toward the experience or education you need to gain confidence in this area.

Day 3

Measure Your Confidence Quotient

> My confidence has grown in direct correlation with my closeness to God. Before I came to God wholeheartedly, my confidence was only in myself and my ability. For me, this manifested quite often in guilt feelings as my mistakes multiplied. Guilt is a major confidence killer.
>
> —Michael, 43

Have you ever noticed that life experience and time have a way of causing you to see former insecurities and doubts in a new light? You may still be working through insecurities and doubts in some areas, but I bet there are other areas where you have found victory. How did you overcome those doubts? What did it take for you to let go of your insecurities?

As we continue this first week of the program, it's important to get clear about where you are lacking in confidence. By identifying specifically the most persistent issues for you, you can better use this book and take measurable steps toward overcoming those issues. I have created this Confidence Quotient (CQ) Assessment to help you see how and where you lack confidence in the five key areas of life. This isn't a test, but a tool, and you can come back to it often to measure your progress and to determine what you may want to work on next as you grow personally, professionally, and spiritually.

Place a check mark (✓) next to each statement below that is true for you.

Confidence Quotient (CQ) Assessment

Relationships

- ☐ I'm uncomfortable saying no to a request even if I really don't want to do it. I sometimes make up a story or feel guilty for saying no.
- ☐ I'm not as confident in myself when I'm not in a romantic relationship.
- ☐ I compare myself (my looks, possessions, financial situation, and so on) with others in order to measure my value, importance, or progress.
- ☐ I sometimes go out of my way to avoid meeting or being introduced to new people.
- ☐ I am shy.
- ☐ I'm easily influenced by the opinions of others.
- ☐ I sometimes feel intimidated in the presence of people I perceive as more successful than I am.
- ☐ I don't speak up for myself, and I sometimes find myself mulling over what I "should have said" during a previous conversation.
- ☐ I find it very difficult to speak before a group.

- ☐ I don't feel respected in all my relationships. If I'm not treated respectfully, I still allow the relationship to continue without changing the frequency or type of interactions.

Finances

- ☐ I'm not confident in my ability to make good financial decisions.
- ☐ In the last twelve months, I've purchased things to impress others.
- ☐ If I lost my job today, I wouldn't be able to recover very quickly from my job loss.
- ☐ I sometimes have difficulty asking for money that is owed me by a family member, friend, customer, or employer.
- ☐ I earn a below-average salary for my industry and position, and I'm underpaid for someone of my experience and background.
- ☐ I rarely end negotiations for a salary or contract feeling good about the energy I'll need to put in to earn the agreed-upon amount.
- ☐ I don't know how much money I have or how much I owe. I'm always guessing because I have no spending plan or budget.
- ☐ I measure my self-worth by my salary or my net worth.
- ☐ I'm not financially comfortable with my friends: I feel pressured to keep up with them or spend money I don't have.
- ☐ I spend money hastily without considering what really matters to me.

Work

If you don't work for pay, answer these questions about your primary vocation or activities.

- ☐ I sometimes doubt my ability to do my job well.
- ☐ I'm not confident in my ability to land another job in a reasonable amount of time should this one go away for any reason.

- ☐ In my current work, I am unable to fulfill my true professional potential.
- ☐ My special gifts and talents would be better used elsewhere. I don't feel I am where I am supposed to be at this point in my life.
- ☐ My co-workers doubt or discourage me professionally. They are concerned with "picking up the slack," double-checking my work, or showing me how to do things.
- ☐ I don't feel good about myself when I'm at work.
- ☐ If I want to advance in my career, I'd have to make a lot of changes to make it happen.
- ☐ I'm worried about people at work making me look bad because their performance or productivity is better than mine.
- ☐ I don't typically take initiative on projects and opportunities in my work.
- ☐ I have doubts about how good my professional reputation is.

Health and Physical Appearance

- ☐ I don't feel good about how I look.
- ☐ I'm unsure of what it takes to maintain a healthy body, or I have not been able to trust myself to make needed changes.
- ☐ I sometimes make excuses or am embarrassed by what I eat.
- ☐ I don't feel good about how I take care of myself.
- ☐ There's something about my appearance that I feel I need to hide.
- ☐ I sometimes ignore signs that I may be getting sick or that I have a health challenge I need to address.
- ☐ My appearance detracts from my confidence more than it boosts my confidence.
- ☐ I have at least one habit that negatively impacts my health, but I am not actively seeking help or a solution.

- □ There's at least one preventable disease in my family history, and I am engaging in habits that put me at risk of getting that disease.
- □ My home environment is sometimes stressful.

Spiritual Life

- □ I'm unclear about the purpose of my life.
- □ When I have a problem, my *first* source of guidance is someone in my life who will listen and give me some advice.
- □ After the mistakes I've made and sometimes continue to make, I'm unsure about God's love for me.
- □ There's at least one area of my life in which I have felt God leading me to step out in faith, yet I haven't done so.
- □ When I set out to accomplish a goal, doubt sometimes keeps me from reaching it.
- □ I still need to be healed from a past wound in my life.
- □ I sometimes doubt my ability to make wise decisions.
- □ I'm a perfectionist. I'm not comfortable with making mistakes or potentially getting it wrong.
- □ I don't step out in faith if I might fail.
- □ My faith in myself is the foundation of my confidence.

______ Write down your total number of checked answers here. (The fewer the checked spaces, the higher your CQ.)

As I've talked with and heard from hundreds of people about their perspectives on their own confidence levels, I've identified four general experiences. Which of these four experiences best describes your confidence?

- *Lack of Confidence.* Forget the superficial, circumstantial category. Nothing seems to cause you to feel confident. Some people may call you shy, but you know it's much deeper than that. It's time to work on your self-esteem, and I'm honored to walk with you on this journey as you let go of fear, doubt, and insecurity and begin to move toward authentic confidence.

- *Circumstantial Confidence.* You feel confident based on circumstances, people, or material items. The foundation of your confidence is based on where you live, who you know, how you look, and other superficialities that have no permanence. Circumstantial confidence is actually not confidence at all, but you can appear very confident. You know how to control your image, and you have worked it to your advantage. Consider yourself circumstantially confident if you lack confidence because you don't have what you believe will give it to you: a spouse, material possessions, status, or popularity, to name a few.
- *Partial Confidence.* You find yourself feeling confident in one area of your life but lacking confidence in another. While you may be authentically confident in your relationships, for example, you cannot seem to tap into that same authentic confidence in your professional life.
- *Authentic Confidence.* Your confidence is based on who you are rather than what you do. It is a combination of self-confidence built on a foundation of faith. You have faith in God's promises, you trust Him in all things, and you allow your inner spirit to emerge in everyday interactions and activities. Your authentic confidence permeates everything you do, both personally and professionally. Everything you communicate exudes confidence. You prepare for and pursue excellence. You maximize your talent, education, and skills as you feel led, and you trust God to do the rest.

Confidence Prayer

Thank You, God, for opening my eyes today to some of the ways I lack confidence. Show me what areas You want me to focus on first. Help me strengthen my confidence day by day, despite longstanding doubts, persistent insecurities, or a lack of encouragement from those I wish would encourage me. Open my eyes to myself, and grant me the focus to make needed changes. I don't want partial confidence or circumstantial confidence. Lord, give me authentic confidence.

Confidence Journal

What statements on the Confidence Quotient Assessment were you most bothered about checking off? Write down those statements. What will you need to do differently in order for these statements to no longer be true for you?

Confidence Builder

Today, choose a simple action step you've lacked the confidence to take, such as asking for an opportunity, introducing yourself to someone, or setting a boundary in a relationship—and take that action before the day ends. You can do it!

Day 4

Be Honest

> I think our culture encourages people to appear that they have it all together in every area of their life. It liberated me when I became completely honest about what was wrong.
>
> —JENNA, 29

Lisa had a string of three romantic relationships in five years that left her frustrated with men. She had a lot going for her, but she never felt comfortable with men who seemed to have as much going for them as she did.

Truth be told, Lisa was intimidated by them.

She seemed so together on the outside, but she always felt like a fake. Nonsupportive family members reminded her regularly, "You shouldn't think that because you got your education that you're somehow better than everyone else. Those new friends you have don't say it, but they look down on you because you don't come from a background like theirs."

It wasn't true, but the seeds of doubt were planted, and Lisa had begun to water them. Because of the attitudes of so many in her family, she felt conflicted about her educational and professional success. When she dated men in her professional circles, she always seemed uneasy. She wondered what they were thinking about her, whether they thought she was good enough. She pressured herself to the point that she felt like she had to perform—to say the right things and behave the right way.

Even though she might enjoy a relationship with a man, she couldn't be herself for fear she'd be found out and rejected. She told herself that she lacked confidence with these men because they thought they were better than she was.

Truthfully, *she* thought they were better than she was. It was a lie, of course, but being honest about it meant facing deep-rooted, longstanding issues in her life. She was comfortable with men who had little ambition and didn't seem to go out of their way to be with her. They were safe and nonthreatening.

When something isn't working in a person's life, sometimes the first reaction is to look at all the external issues that may be the cause: "The people at work aren't being fair" or "No one is going to pay me any more for my services, so there is no need to ask" or "I can't bring that up with him right now because I know he can't handle it."

Often, when you peel back the layers, you find there's more to a story than meets the eye. That's true of your own story as well.

A lack of confidence is not always caused by what you think it is caused by. So I challenge you to dig deep and be honest about the range of emotions, insecurities, or doubts that are really going through your mind.

Jesus said, "You shall know the truth, and the truth shall make you free" (John 8:32, NKJV). Both the truth of God's Word and the truth of your situation will set you free. But if you allow fear to keep you from exploring your truth, you'll never heal from the wounds of the past or move forward in confidence. Don't pretend you're okay when you're not. Burying feelings that are alive doesn't cause them to die. It causes them to fester into insecurities, doubt, and a lack of confidence.

At times there are good reasons why you don't feel confident. As a personal and professional life coach, I've observed these reasons:

- You're not prepared.
- You're out of God's will.
- You're pushing something to happen before its time.
- You're making an emotional decision rather than a spiritually guided one.
- You're buying into lies or stereotypes that dissuade you.
- You're basing your confidence on superficialities.
- You're too busy comparing yourself to others.
- You've set for yourself the unachievable goal of perfection.
- You've set a goal that you are not yet ready to achieve.
- You haven't taken full responsibility for your actions.
- You're trying to do something that God doesn't mean for you to do—something outside your purpose, gifts, talents, and passion.

Admitting that one of these statements describes you can be unsettling. It can force you to see yourself in a new light. When you realize that your image of yourself as a self-confident, got-it-all-figured-out person might not be accurate, your foundation shifts. But instead of reacting in panic to the unfamiliar sensations, work with God to build a stronger foundation.

You can deal with your lack of authentic confidence and allow God to take you to a higher level of spiritual maturity and growth, or you can ignore it. The latter, of course, means living in bondage to an issue that

God has given you the power to overcome. In *Listen to Your Life,* I introduced the concept of self-curiosity.

Through self-curiosity, you learn from mistakes and envy, from happiness and disappointment. Over time, challenges that once seemed insurmountable become steppingstones to success. Rather than running from issues, you face them with courage and say, "You know what? You've been here too long. I'm tired of you stealing my joy. It's time for you to go." We grow by questioning our actions, noticing our intentions, and seeking our healthiest mental, spiritual, and emotional state of being.

Whenever you delve into deeper questions, you will encounter resistance. It's fear. Everything you do in life is out of either fear or love. Love for others, love for God, love for yourself, and passion for something are examples of the love that motivates you to do certain things. It makes me sad, though, that so many people operate daily from a place of fear—fear of pain, rejection, failure, commitment, ridicule, being wrong, or even being successful and handling the responsibility that comes with it.

Yet 1 John 4:18 promises, "There is no fear in love. But perfect love drives out fear, because fear has to do with punishment. The one who fears is not made perfect in love." I challenge you to notice your fears and face them. Ask yourself:

- *What am I afraid of?*
- *Is that true?*
- *What am I afraid will happen if…?*
- *What's the likelihood of that?*
- *What if it does happen?*
- *What can I do about this now?*

Ask yourself the probing questions that come to mind. Then, after you've explored the source of your fear, ask yourself an action question:

- *How can I move forward?*
- *What does God want me to do here?*
- *What's a small but meaningful step I could take in the right direction?*
- *What is a big change I could make now?*

We sometimes go overboard telling people, "You can do anything you put your mind to." Authentic confidence isn't about doing anything you put your mind to. Instead, it's about doing everything that God has for you to do. There are things we can put our minds to that have nothing to do with our purpose in life or God's will for us.

For instance, Philippians 4:13, quoted often, says:

> I can do everything through him who gives me strength.

But it's easy to quote a scripture out of context. Let's look at the verses before it and read it in context:

> I rejoice greatly in the Lord that at last you have renewed your concern for me. Indeed, you have been concerned, but you had no opportunity to show it. (verse 10)

> I am not saying this because I am in need, for I have learned to be content whatever the circumstances. I know what it is to be in need, and I know what it is to have plenty. I have learned the secret of being content in any and every situation, whether well fed or hungry, whether living in plenty or in want. (verses 11–12)

> I can do everything through him who gives me strength. (verse 13)

Paul was writing to the Philippians, from whom he accepted gifts that were offered to him as their minister. He mentioned in an earlier book (1 Corinthians 9) that he didn't accept gifts from the Corinthians because he didn't want to be accused of teaching and preaching God's word for the sole purpose of making money.

So Paul was doing God's work, and that's not always easy. At times, he struggled to have his needs met. Yet he learned to be content and to persevere through those times because he could do everything through Christ who was the source of his strength. Anything you set out to do within God's will for your life, you can do. Even those things that feel absolutely impossible—and take you beyond your comfort zone—are possible.

"With man this is impossible, but with God all things are possible," Jesus said in Matthew 19:26. Philippians 4:13 is about being able and willing to persevere in doing God's will because Christ is the source of your strength.

I want you to have the confidence to let go of those situations in your life that God no longer means for you to be involved in. Perhaps there's a peer group that you want desperately to be a part of, but it is not a good fit for you. Still, it represents something to you that would make you feel more important or worthy in some way. *God wants you to focus on Him as the source of your value.*

Perhaps it's a relationship you're clinging to that saps your energy or self-respect. You hold on for some reason, yet it's chipping away at you daily. *It's time to let go.*

You may lack financial confidence. It's time to pursue a new job or a new career, or perhaps you just need to ask your current employer for more compensation. *Be willing to let go of the old in order to enter God-glorifying situations instead.*

Confidence Prayer

God, show me Your will for my life. Strengthen my faith and my belief that I can do all things that You want me to do. With You, all things are possible! Thank You for that amazing promise.

Confidence Journal

In what area of your life do you lack confidence and feel God leading you to dig deeper to find your truth and face it? What are you afraid might be the truth? Be specific. Once you answer that question, decide whether that really is the truth. What does God want you to do about that truth in order for you to gain authentic confidence?

Confidence Builder

Today, implement this confidence tip: Make sure you speak from your diaphragm. Lower your voice when you speak. A lower pitch feels and sounds more confident and trustworthy.

Day 5

Face Your Fears and Insecurities

> I take one challenge a week to step out of my comfort zone. Sometimes it's a matter of standing firm on my business rates, and sometimes it's a matter of speaking up for myself in difficult conversations. I feel confident when I overcome my fears.
>
> —Lisa, 46

God knows we feel fear. Throughout the Bible, a particular verse is repeated in multiple books. I first noticed it when the Lord spoke to Moses's protégé Joshua. Moses had died, and Joshua was left with the historic and long-awaited task of leading the Israelites into the Promised Land. Moses climbed to the top of Mount Nebo in Moab and saw a glimpse of the Promised Land, but he never saw his people step into that land. The Lord says to Moses in Deuteronomy 34:4,

> This is the land I promised on oath to Abraham, Isaac and Jacob when I said, "I will give it to your descendants." I have let you see it with your eyes, but you will not cross over into it.

The scripture goes on to say:

> Now Joshua son of Nun was filled with the spirit of wisdom because Moses had laid his hands on him. So the Israelites listened to him and did what the LORD had commanded Moses.
>
> Since then, no prophet has risen in Israel like Moses, whom the LORD knew face to face, who did all those miraculous signs and wonders the LORD sent him to do in Egypt—to Pharaoh and to all his officials and to his whole land. For no one has ever shown the mighty power or performed the awesome deeds that Moses did in the sight of all Israel. (verses 9–12)

Imagine how intimidated Joshua must have felt, stepping up to fill shoes that simply could not and would not ever be fully filled. But did you know that God can use you in a mighty way despite the fact that you may not look like or be like those who have gone before you and succeeded? Joshua was prepared for the task, but he was afraid. He had always had his mentor and leader, Moses. He hadn't had to make the leadership decisions. But now there was only him. It was a moment that would define his character. The Lord must have known Joshua was afraid because He reassured him:

> No one will be able to stand up against you all the days of your life. As I was with Moses, so I will be with you; I will never leave you nor forsake you.

> Be strong and courageous, because you will lead these people to inherit the land I swore to their forefathers to give them. (Joshua 1:5–6)

Notice specifically the command, "Be strong and courageous." If we were never to feel fear, God would not command Joshua to be strong and courageous. You don't need courage unless you are fearful. The command is repeated two more times in the next three verses:

> Be strong and very courageous. (verse 7)

> Have I not commanded you? Be strong and courageous. Do not be terrified; do not be discouraged, for the LORD your God will be with you wherever you go. (verse 9)

Variations on these words about strength and courage can be found repeatedly throughout the Bible. Clearly, God understands that in our own humanity we will feel fear. The enemy will persist in tempting us with thoughts that provoke fear.

What's your reaction to fear? When fearful, most people almost instinctively pretend courage, run away, or try to hide. In fact, most reactions to fear are so automatic and common that you may not even have identified a lack of confidence as fear. Yet a lack of confidence is created by an abundance of fear. It's fear that creates insecurities and fuels doubt.

Our job is not to pretend fear doesn't exist or to run and hide from it; our job is to be strong and courageous in unearthing the fear so we can confront and conquer it. This process begins with getting to the essence of your being and acknowledging the reality of your fears. You can overcome your fears. Let me restate that: God is with you wherever you go, and He will enable you to overcome your fears.

This means we need to start unearthing the parts of us that are underdeveloped or that have difficulties speaking up, feeling confident, and being bold about moving toward our visions. The journey is different for each of us, depending on our experiences. For some, growth in a particular area was stunted when we were young. Others lost confidence due to an experience in adulthood. Whatever your situation, you can acknowledge the pain or damage that was caused, then move forward by admitting and facing your fears.

So, in order to build authentic confidence, you must first get to the heart of why you lack confidence in a particular area. What is it you're afraid of? Who will you need to become in order to push through your fears? As you unearth your fears, you can face them, eliminate them, and make room for the real you to emerge—confidently.

For example, fear (leading to a lack of confidence) is often rooted in the lies you have been told, the lies that you chose to believe. Perhaps long ago someone suggested that you were unattractive, and you believed that lie. No matter how beautiful you are, you don't feel beautiful, and it shows in your body language and attitude. You must allow God to help you replace this lie with truth.

"God has not given us a spirit of fear, but of power and of love and of a sound mind," is an often quoted scripture about fear (2 Timothy 1:7, NKJV). But some have misunderstood it to mean that having fear is wrong, even sinful, and they don a cloak of shame about the fear they've experienced. I'm not here to berate you about feeling fear. You feel what you feel. Where we get into trouble with fear is when we allow the fact that we feel it to dictate how we choose to behave. You can feel something and not act on that feeling. In fact, in order to become authentically confident, it is essential that you do not act on the fear that you feel at any given moment.

In life coaching, there's a phrase often used called "coaching the essence." There are three elements that I might be coaching at any given time:

- what (vision, goal, objective)
- how (steps to achieve the vision, goal, objective)
- who (the core of what drives this person, what his or her spirit is longing for, what needs are or are not being met that hinder progress)

The "who" is the essence. While most people know what they want and how to get it, many are ineffective despite that knowledge. Exploring deeper aspects of who you are and what really drives you is the process that has the greatest power to move you forward in a sustained way.

Coach University, the program I went through to be trained as a coach, defines *essence* this way: "Fundamental nature, inherent characteristics. The core heart and soul of the person you are coaching."

When I'm coaching people, they will often tell me about a specific goal they would like to accomplish. They may want to prepare and build confidence to achieve the goal successfully, so they hire a coach to show them "what" needs to be done and "how" to do it. But if the coaching revolves completely around the required steps, these people often find themselves still stuck. They become frustrated as weeks—sometimes months—pass and they can't figure out why they aren't moving forward when they know what to do.

I'd like to share with you some questions that will help you coach your essence. When you're lacking confidence in a particular area—whether in a relationship, at work, or on a goal for which you are losing steam—the natural tendency is to focus on *what you need to do* to move forward rather than *who you need to be* to move forward. Doing what you need to do may seem to work for you in the short term, but you'll wear yourself out and need to pump yourself up again to find motivation.

Focusing instead on who you need to become—in other words, fully realizing the essence of who you truly are and the potential God has placed within you—will fuel and sustain transformation and personal growth. So here are some self-coaching questions you can ask yourself in order to get in touch with your essence:

- *Honestly, do I really want to do this? If so, why? What's my purpose in it?*
- *What does my inner voice—the voice of the Holy Spirit—tell me?*
- *What's keeping me from standing up fully and confidently in this situation?*
- *What am I afraid of?*
- *What doubts hinder me right now? What's the truth about each of those doubts?*
- *Who will I need to become in order to achieve the goal or vision set before me?*
- *What will it feel like to stand fully in who I am?*
- *How do I want to feel in the situation in which I am lacking confidence?*
- *What will I have to do differently in order for success to come more easily?*
- *What opportunity for growth is before me right now?*
- *What will it take for me to embrace this opportunity for growth?*

Confidence Prayer

John 8:32 says, "You shall know the truth, and the truth shall make you free." Help me get to the heart of the fears that diminish my confidence so that I may rise above them. Allow the right questions to come to mind, and help me answer them with honesty and confidence.

Confidence Journal

Which one or two of the self-coaching questions listed at the end of this chapter do you find most compelling? Explain.

Confidence Builder

Today, in keeping with your intention to be honest, work on connecting heart to heart with the people you speak to. Look them in the eye. Be in the moment with them rather than thinking about your next activity or a previous one.

Day 6

Free Yourself from Your Past

> I'm building a business and find myself carrying all the baggage from past failed businesses, plus negative remarks from former employers, parents, and teachers. It's a constant reminder that I'm not as confident as I should be.
>
> —LOGAN, 33

I don't believe in becoming stuck in the past, but I do believe in learning from it. You can be stuck in the past and not even realize it. For example, what habit or coping strategy did you learn from a negative experience in your past that you continue to use today?

I learned from a painful period in my past, and I hope that you can see your own struggle in my story and then experience the freedom that can come from connecting the dots.

When I was twenty-four years old, I began to trace my personal history to uncover the buried but unhealed wounds that persisted in my life. An unexpected romantic breakup had left me feeling unsure of myself, for the first time I could remember. In fact, my reaction was so intense—crying at the drop of a hat, insomnia, no appetite whatsoever—that it occurred to me that maybe more than the breakup was breaching the surface of my emotions.

To me the relationship seemed to be cruising along happily. But that was when he came to the realization that we weren't meant for each other. I thought he was coming over so we could go see a movie, but his first words were, "We need to talk."

Nothing good ever seems to come after those words, does it?

His tone was direct and casual: "I really like you. You're everything I want in a woman. But I don't love you, and I don't think I ever will. I mean I think I'm in love with what you represent, but if you worked at McDonald's or something, I don't think I'd be with you."

Ouch.

Well, at least he told the truth. It hurt at the time, but he actually did me a big favor. There's no need to have relationships that are not authentic. Of course, that's hindsight speaking. In that moment, I couldn't believe what I was hearing. I was confused, and in the weeks to come, all sorts of feelings of abandonment began to bubble up. Never before had I questioned my self-esteem, and I certainly couldn't recall ever feeling so not in control. I didn't know I'd felt abandoned before, but my ex's actions prompted an epiphany. They intensified a fear I had buried—of being left alone or being rejected.

I don't recall that anyone had ever broken up with me before, and at first I believed I was being punished for breaking up with the love of my life a couple of years earlier—the man God would later bring back into my life because he was the one I was meant to marry. I thought perhaps God wanted me to feel what he had felt. The guilt was intense.

I now realize that the breakup triggered the devastating emotions that had emerged upon my parents' separation when I was thirteen years old. My mother had moved one hundred miles away to Cheyenne, Wyoming, for a job promotion. One month after her move, on a sunny afternoon, my parents called me into their bedroom. "We need to talk," they said.

My mother said that she and my father were getting a divorce.

The words blindsided me. I felt like I was in a dream. Surely I would wake up shortly in a sweat, then be able to drift back off to sleep and stumble upon a much more positive dream.

"You aren't surprised, are you?" I recall her asking.

I was perplexed by the question. My parents argued, but divorce had never once crossed my mind. (They were separated for four years before they actually divorced.) I'd never imagined my life would be any different than it was the moment before they called me into the bedroom.

I was too young to fully understand the scope of emotions I was feeling at that time, but in the moment of my own breakup, the emotions that I'd minimized—even ignored—for all those years came rushing in. I knew instinctively that the emotions were steeped in my past and that it was time to deal with them.

I feel blessed to have grown up in a household with two loving parents. I was close to both my mom and dad. We ate dinner together most nights, went to the movies, traveled together, and created a lot of good memories. My parents were born in the same town, and their families were interconnected. In fact, when my paternal grandmother left the doctor's office on the day she found out she was pregnant with my father, she headed out to get her hair done by her beautician—who was my maternal grandmother, not yet pregnant with my mom. (That wouldn't happen for another year.) My maternal grandmother is the first person she told that she was pregnant with my father.

Amazing.

I felt ashamed that my parents were separating. But we kept our family matters private, and I didn't talk about it much. Even though I talked to my mom daily and she visited nearly every week, I missed her deeply.

In the previous seven years, my father had lost his mother, father, and brother; it was a difficult time. I'd spent every summer since the age of three at my father's parents' house. I focused on school, sports, and extracurricular activities, which in retrospect gave me a place to feel confident and stable. Those were areas of my life I could control.

After two years of living with my father after my parents' separation, I moved to live with my mother. I was fifteen. It was the last time I lived with my dad. I was sad. Angry. Afraid. Ashamed. Uncertain.

On the last night in our house where I lived with my dad, I buried my face in my pillow as tears streamed down my cheeks. I covered my head with my rose-colored comforter with its cream-colored lace trim. I'd had the matching canopy bed since we lived in Florida. My parents brought it home from Sears when I was about four years old. It had followed us to Germany and now to Colorado. The rose-colored comforter was new, though. I'd picked it out with my dad before our house was completed—and this was the first house my parents owned. We'd visited it every day while it was being built. We'd been in it for five years, and now we were saying good-bye. We would never live in a house again together as a family.

Nine years would pass before I realized the depth of my anguish over this loss. It wasn't just losing my house. I wasn't just losing my home. I was losing my family.

Other kids' parents get divorced, but not mine, I thought.

Why do we always think bad things are supposed to happen to everyone else, but not to us?

With their separation when I was thirteen, I began to lose an inner confidence, a loss that I ignored and covered well. I often felt inadequate. I didn't show it on the outside, but I felt like everyone around me had more confidence than I did. Not only did I feel they had more, but I began to turn that feeling into a *belief* that they would always have more.

Have you ever felt inadequate? It's not something most people who feel that way will readily admit or discuss. Feeling inadequate, however, prompts countless poor decisions. It can cause you to shrink from your potential, place others on a pedestal, and concern yourself with racking up external accolades that will allow you to measure up. Of course achievements and accolades can be good things, but you'll exhaust yourself if you consume yourself with accumulating them.

My experiences that resulted from the divorce of my parents became a wounded place for me. I believe I subconsciously internalized my mother's move to take a promotion, my parents' focus on their marital challenges, and the subsequent and wrenching transition as indicators that I was not significant.

If I were significant enough, wouldn't my parents have worked it out after all? was the question of my subconscious.

As an adult, you recognize the fallacy of this thinking, but to a child, it seems very rational. The problem is that too many of us interpret the trials that happen to us as we are growing up, but we never reinterpret those experiences after we reach adulthood. What released me from these childhood feelings of abandonment was having a conversation about my feelings with each of my parents.

At age twenty-four, I finally asked questions I'd never asked before, and I shared the feelings I'd kept to myself. All those years I had been afraid to bring any of it up, as though I didn't have a right to be hurt, angry, or frustrated. Both my mom and dad were loving and honest in their responses, and for the first time as an adult, I could process what had happened to me when I was a child. I could empathize with where they were in their lives at the time of the separation. And I could see how they had protected me as best they could at that time.

What overriding feeling is undermining your confidence?

For me, it was the feeling that the best things were reserved for others, not for me. Despite the fact that great things were happening to me frequently, I still had a persistent feeling that I was somehow behind the curve and that my success was limited.

Of course, as long as you believe that kind of lie, you will behave in ways that fulfill that lie and make it a truth in your life. My past held clues about this belief, though. We lived in a terrific area, and by middle-class standards, we did great. But I went to school with many students whose families did even better financially. Everything in life is relative. If I'd lived just a few miles away, I would probably have felt like the privileged one.

As my experience may help you see, by looking into the past, we can find clues to issues that are plaguing us and undermining our confidence in the present. If you look into your past but cannot connect the dots between the events of your life, pray and ask God to reveal those connections to you.

Don't worry if you don't get this kind of insight as quickly as you'd like. You don't have to know why you do the things you do to know that they're not working for you. If you get stuck focusing on the "why," you may never move forward. Understanding why can help you respond better and can even help you heal, but it's not necessary to changing your behavior. In order to change your behavior, you simply need to identify the beliefs that limit you and undermine your self-esteem and self-confidence.

Confidence Prayer

Lord, I don't want to get stuck in the past. I want to be like Paul who said in Philippians 3:13–14, "Forgetting those things which are behind and reaching forward to those things which are ahead, I press toward the goal for the prize of the upward call of God in Christ Jesus." Help me glean clues from my past so that I may understand myself better and break my self-sabotaging habits. I want to be free so that I will have the confidence to serve You fully.

Confidence Journal

Write about what experience from your past taints your thought process today, causing you to make decisions from a position of fear or insecurity rather than courage and confidence. What steps do you need to take to free yourself from this chapter of your past?

Confidence Builder

Today, when you walk, don't rush. Feel the confidence that emerges from a purposeful yet unhurried glide.

Day 7

Escape the Overcompensation Rut

> I think I'm addicted to achievement. Goal setting is second nature for me—at school, at work, with my money. And I love growing and exceeding my expectations. It builds my confidence, but sometimes I'm just so exhausted from constantly racing from one goal to the next.
>
> —Laura, 33

After my first year of college, I felt dumb. My academic confidence had spiraled down the drain, along with my grades. I'd spent nearly an entire year on academic probation with a GPA hovering below 1.5, so I decided to leave the Air Force Academy and try to find myself elsewhere. My parents had divorced that year, and my mother had moved to Monterey, California—a state I'd always thought of as cool and adventurous. So I headed to sunny California to go to a small college in Monterey while figuring out what university I would transfer to later.

When I arrived in Monterey, I actually questioned my ability to even pass my classes. I projected the failures I had experienced at the Air Force Academy onto my present academic life. I wanted to prove I was still an exceptional student despite my miserable failures during my first year of college. So I shifted into overdrive.

During those nine months, I took twenty-one semester hours in the fall and eighteen in the spring—while working part-time. I transferred to Florida State University in the summer, which, despite my first-year college struggles, offered me a tuition scholarship and the opportunity to finish college without taking out any student loans.

Then I proceeded along my overdriven path, intensely studying the course schedule and university policies to determine how quickly I could finish school. I didn't realize it at the time, but I was on a fast track because I was overcompensating for my first-year failure.

If I graduate early, then surely that means I'm not dumb, I reasoned subconsciously. And I did. Taking eighteen semester hours during the summer term, I graduated in August 1993 with a bachelor's degree in international affairs. I imagined myself an international corporate attorney, but as I raced toward graduation and researched what I would be doing as an attorney, I decided that I would not be passionate about a career in law. Nearby Florida A&M University was beginning a graduate program in its journalism school, and I decided to apply.

Two weeks after graduating from FSU, I began work on my master's degree. Just as I had done at FSU, I designed an academic track that would allow me to finish quickly.

Sixteen months later, I graduated. I was twenty-one years old with a master's degree, and I had just begun to truly enjoy school. I could now prove that although I had failed at seventeen and eighteen years old, I was not dumb.

But to whom was I proving this?

My parents didn't think I was dumb. Nor my friends. I suppose I was trying to prove something to my biggest critic: me.

I reached my goal of early graduation, but then I realized that perhaps reaching the goal would have been less important if I'd focused more on enjoying my journey.

Of course, when you overcompensate for your insecurities and past failures, relaxing and enjoying the journey is not your top priority. And often your failures are a much bigger deal in your mind than they are to anyone else.

I rarely talked about my academy experience until I wrote about it in my first book—eight years after I left. This "failure" that was such a big deal in my mind was not the big deal I had long imagined it to be. In fact, numerous people thanked me for sharing that story because it helped them see that the things they consider failures are often closed doors that help them change direction and move them toward something they are passionate about.

Overcompensation and overachievement often go hand in hand. Because they're habits that can reap accolades and recognition from others, it is easy to fall into a never-ending cycle of overachieving in order to compensate for your perceived shortcomings.

To be clear, I think achievement is generally a good thing. That is, achievement within God's will for you and according to His timing for you. This is very different from an appetite for achievement that is never satisfied—an appetite that fuels a cycle you can never escape because no matter what you achieve, it's not enough.

Perhaps you've never experienced this overachievement rut in the academic world or your work life, but you experience it in your relationships or in your financial affairs. To compensate for past failures, you go overboard to win the approval and affection of a loved one or friend. Or to compensate for a past when you lacked basic necessities, you compensate now by overspending or underspending. Either you overspend to ensure that you never feel poor again, or you hoard money and refuse to spend it for fear you'll run out and once again won't have enough.

The key to both freedom and confidence is accepting your past failures, mistakes, and regrets. When you change your perceptions of what those aspects of your past mean, you can change your beliefs about what you must do—if anything—to compensate for them. After all, the meaning that you assign to the experiences in your life is what generates your response to them.

In my case, I translated low grades to mean I was dumb. After all, I couldn't possibly be as smart as I thought I was if I'd failed some classes and got Cs and Ds in others, right? Those grades shook my confidence and my belief in my abilities.

Could the guys who gave me a hard time in high school have been right when they said it was a fluke that I was accepted to such a prestigious school? I wondered. *Were the male cadets right who insisted it was easier for me to get in because I was a woman and a minority?*

These questions held meaning for me—meaning that wasn't necessarily rooted in truth. My reaction to the meaning was to prove to myself that I was "smart." So I assigned a meaning to finishing college and graduate school early. I decided that if I could achieve those goals, that accomplishment would outweigh my first-year academic failures.

The truth was simple: the academy wasn't the place for me. I wasn't passionate about it. It wasn't my path. And that's okay. We all have something for which our greatest gifts can emerge.

The military was not the environment where my greatest gifts could emerge. If I had understood that simple truth in the early 1990s, I wouldn't have poured so much energy into compensating for my perceived failure.

In what area of your life have you interpreted certain events in a way that undermines your confidence and/or makes you try to compensate for what happened?

____

____

Now reframe those events and experiences so that there is no need for you to compensate for them. (A longtime friend might help you do this.)

____

____

____

In case you are wondering if you overcompensate in any area of your life, consider these ways in which the habit of overcompensating can manifest itself in your life. Notice whether any of these statements describe you.

- You're always trying to prove something to someone—or to yourself.
- You go overboard to lavish others with praise or gifts to win their favor.
- You say, "I'm sorry," for things that don't warrant an apology. It's a phrase in your vocabulary that is overused.
- You buy things to impress, fit in, win favor, or accommodate others' expectations, whether or not you can actually afford them.

- You're constantly seeking more credentials that will validate your qualifications—whether or not God has led you to seek those credentials.
- You speak or behave the way you think you should in certain environments rather than just being yourself.
- You always have to be the person in control. You don't trust others to be in control.
- You work too hard and too much.
- You race to the finish line of every project in order to cross it off your list, but you fail to enjoy the journey.
- You go to the extreme with anything and everything—diets, exercise, spending, saving, talking, not speaking up, working, winning others' approval, overachieving, or even underachieving.

Overcompensation is a form of bondage that is fueled by fear. God wants you free from the extremes of life and balanced in your approach to life. Experiences happen that breed insecurities, but you can choose how you respond to the insecurities stemming from past failures, mistakes, and doubts. You don't have to be controlled by your feelings. You are going to doubt yourself sometimes. You'll feel insecure sometimes. But feeling insecure and acting on that insecurity are two separate issues.

Beginning today, you can choose to respond differently to the urge to overcompensate for your perceived shortcomings. When you do, you'll gain confidence in fully accepting who you are and where you've been without the need to make up for what you think is missing. God's grace is sufficient to deliver us from insecurity, and His wisdom is more than enough to teach us the life lessons that can be learned from the negative aspects of our past. Focus less on your shortcomings and more on His perfect plan for your life—a plan which incorporates your imperfections.

Confidence Prayer

I'm tired of overcompensating and overachieving. It's exhausting. Jesus, Your example was a perfect one. You fulfilled Your calling and didn't give in to pressure to constantly do more and wear Yourself out. Help me trust that I'm already enough. Help me resist the temptation to prove myself to the world and instead to focus more on proving my trust in You.

Confidence Journal

In what areas of life do you overcompensate for an insecurity, past failure, or mistake that has undermined your confidence? With what behaviors do you overcompensate? Be specific.

Confidence Builder

Today, identify one specific way that you'll stop overcompensating. Either choose something to let go of, or identify an attitude shift you can make.

Day 8

Have Faith

> With age and a splash of spiritual maturity, it has truly become easier for me not to sweat the small stuff—or the big stuff, for that matter. I learned to relax once I placed my confidence in God and not in myself. Hallelujah!
>
> —Sherry, 51

When I began to grow spiritually, my confidence changed in a profound way. Its foundation shifted. That's perhaps the best way I can describe it. I believed in God before, but as I began to draw nearer to Him, my confidence became less about me and more about Him. When I look back over my life, I'm astonished to see that the most significant occurrences have clearly been divinely orchestrated. And I have full confidence that the most significant things to come will be divinely orchestrated as well.

"Every word of God is flawless," Proverbs 30:5 says. "He is a shield to those who take refuge in him." Our job is to trust God, place our faith in Him only, and follow His nudges and guidance that we sense in our spirits day by day. Those nudges and guidance are the preparation. When you allow God to orchestrate the events of your life, it doesn't mean that you get to sit back and watch. You work and He opens (and sometimes closes) doors. You can be confident that if you live within God's purpose for your life, you will be successful even if you cannot figure out how.

You may not fully understand why you are being led in certain directions, but you can have complete confidence that your life is significant and that every day you can be a vessel for God. After all, you are significant in God's eyes. In every situation—at work, at home, in the greater community—He offers you the opportunity to be His vessel. But you must believe that He can and will use you.

As you know by now, the foundation of authentic confidence is faith in God. And to have faith, you must believe and trust Him. There are two more words we'll get to later, but for now, let's take a deeper look at these three foundational words: *faith, belief,* and *trust.*

Faith is essential to authentic confidence. In fact, I was delightfully surprised when I opened my Webster's dictionary to find a scriptural reference among the definitions and to discover that the first words used to define *confidence* are *belief* and *trust.* The secondary definition talks about being *sure* and *certain*—two words that the writer of Hebrews uses to define faith.

Confidence, according to Webster's definition, is (1) firm belief, trust, reliance, (2) the fact of being or feeling certain; assurance, and (7) Bible object of trust: Proverbs 3:26.

Confident, according to Webster's definition, is (1) full of confidence (a) assured; certain [confident of victory] (b) sure of oneself; self-confident; bold (a confident manner).

Proverbs 3:26 says, "For the LORD will be your confidence and will keep your foot from being snared." The sentence just before this (verse 25) says, "Have no fear of sudden disaster or of the ruin that overtakes the wicked."

I find it encouraging that a worldly dictionary cites the Bible for clarity. Proverbs 3:26 assures us that God is the foundation of our confidence. The TNIV translation says simply, "For the LORD will be at your side and will keep your foot from being snared." It replaces "the LORD will be your confidence" with "the LORD will be at your side." What could give us more confidence than that? God confirms this throughout the Bible. Joshua 1:9 says, "Have I not commanded you? Be strong and courageous. Do not be terrified; do not be discouraged, for the LORD your God will be with you wherever you go." He is with you every step of the way. All you have to do is reach out to Him. "Draw near to God and He will draw near to you," James 4:8 (NKJV) assures us.

Why do you need faith in God to have authentic confidence?

And if the foundation of authentic confidence is faith, then how do we define *faith*? The Bible defines faith clearly: "Now faith is being sure of what we hope for and certain of what we do not see" (Hebrews 11:1).

So in order to have faith, we must hope for something. Indeed, you don't need confidence or faith if you are not hoping for anything. It doesn't take any confidence at all to hope for nothing. It's the fear of not getting what they're hoping for that causes many people to bury or downsize their dreams and to stay inside their comfort zone.

This point is important to understand because hope is essential to your spiritual growth. But you don't need to hope for something that already exists.

For example, if you have a job outside the home, you don't need confidence that the company you work for will hire you. They have already hired you. Before you were hired, though, you needed confidence to get the position. At the point of the interview, you are hoping for the job. You have faith that you can have it. But once you get it, why would you waste your energy to build confidence to get hired?

"Hope that is seen is not hope; for why does one still hope for what he sees? But if we hope for what we do not see, we eagerly wait for it with perseverance" (Romans 8:24–25, NKJV). Faith is about believing that what you hope for is possible. You need confidence that you can build relationships, raise responsible children, succeed professionally, prosper financially, and age healthfully.

These are all things that are yet to come—or, if you have begun to experience them already, they are things that are yet to continue. On your journey, as I'm sure you've noticed, you experience obstacles to realizing your potential. Confidence is essential to successfully overcoming those obstacles. For example, things may be moving along nicely at home or at work, but suddenly trouble comes. It could be a dilemma you've never faced before, and not knowing how to deal with it can cause you to lose confidence.

As the enemy attempts to plant seeds of doubt in your mind or discourage you, and as obstacles arise, God promises that hope will emerge for those who persist through their difficulties. Romans 5:3–5 says, "We also rejoice in our sufferings, because we know that suffering produces perseverance; perseverance, character; and character, hope. And hope does not disappoint us, because God has poured out his love into our hearts by the Holy Spirit, whom he has given us."

When you persevere through difficult circumstances in your life, you develop a richer character. The character you develop gives you hope for the future as you see that you made it through, you are stronger, and God allowed all things to work together for your good (see Romans 8:28).

If you were to receive what you think you want as soon as you want it, you would never develop the character you need to fulfill both your greatest potential and God's unique purpose for your life.

The character that we develop through perseverance is mature. "Consider it pure joy, my brothers, whenever you face trials of many kinds, because you know that the testing of your faith develops perseverance. Perseverance must finish its work so that you may be mature and complete, not lacking anything" (James 1:2–4).

Our character is not truly revealed until we face an obstacle. Pressure demands a reaction. Your character is seen in that reaction. *Is it spiritually mature? Is it sure? Is it faith-filled? Is it certain of what you cannot see right now?*

God wants you to be mature and complete, and obstacles help that happen. You see, it's easy to be confident when everything is going your way. It's much more difficult to be confident when your circumstances do not point to the vision you hope for. Your struggles—even your struggles with doubt, insecurity, fear, self-esteem, or self-confidence—are opportunities for growth. God will give you the wisdom and strength to persevere. The character you develop will give you hope.

In fact, I've found that the more I persevere, the greater my level of hope. When you persevere through difficult times, you see the sheer power and goodness of the Lord. Scriptures come alive in your own life—and you believe the Word on a deeper level. You begin leaning on the Word with greater confidence. You see more clearly God's vision for every area of your life even when there is no physical or otherwise worldly evidence. And you trust that the vision will not fade. It will surely come to life for you if you just hang in there.

"For the vision is yet for an appointed time; but at the end it will speak, and it will not lie. Though it tarries, wait for it [persevere!]; because it will surely come, it will not tarry" (Habakkuk 2:3, NKJV). God's Word is clear. Your job is to believe it!

So "faith is being sure of what we hope for and certain of what we do not see." "What we do not see" refers to the vision for your life, which you do not see in the physical realm but in the spiritual realm. And faith is the foundation of your authentic confidence.

The Bible also says in James 2:26, "As the body without the spirit is dead, so faith without deeds is dead." Confidence empowers your deeds (or actions). Confident people step out in faith when God prompts them to do so. There can be no faith without action. Without deeds, our faith is mere words.

If you truly believe God's Word, you take action based on it. That action demonstrates your confidence. "For a dream comes through much activity, and a fool's voice is known by his many words," Ecclesiastes 5:3 (NKJV) says.

Taking action requires confidence. Talking too much is sometimes a cover-up for not taking action. Action is evidence of confidence. Even baby steps are better than no steps. Each step will build greater confidence.

Consider this illustration: Wherever you are right now, you are literally being held by something. Perhaps it is a desk chair or a comfy sofa. Maybe you are lying in bed or on a lawn chair outdoors. If you are standing up, find a seat for a moment while you read this illustration.

As you sit there, you have confidence in whatever is holding you. If you didn't, you probably wouldn't be comfortable enough to be reading this book. Instead, you'd be unsure and unsteady, thinking about what might go wrong or how you could keep from getting hurt. What gives you the confidence to sit there right now? Is it the brand of the chair? Did someone tell you it was sturdy? How do you know that the foundation beneath you will not cave in? You probably didn't think about any of those things when you sat down. You just trusted that you would be safely supported.

I want you to have confidence in what is holding you—or, rather, in *who* is holding you. God has you in the palm of His hand. You're safe and secure. But you must believe it. You must trust Him just like you're trusting the seat that holds you right now. If you don't believe that God is holding you, you'll seek other means of support and ways of compensating for your lack of confidence.

"Faith comes from hearing the message, and the message is heard through the word of Christ," Romans 10:17 explains. If you are to experience authentic confidence, your faith must come from hearing the Word of God. As you open your heart to hear the Word of God, the message permeates your spirit. "It is with your heart that you believe" (Romans 10:10).

If you welcome God's Word into your heart, it becomes a part of who you are. This is not about head knowledge, reciting scriptures, or going to church. God's Word is ultimately not about what you know, but about who you become in the process of living out the message in your everyday life. To help you hear God's Word better, I want to share a few more scriptures about the faith, trust, hope, and belief that serve as the foundation of authentic confidence:

> We live by faith, not by sight. (2 Corinthians 5:7)

> Do not throw away your confidence; it will be richly rewarded. You need to persevere so that when you have done the will of God, you will receive what he has promised. (Hebrews 10:35–36)

> Without faith it is impossible to please God, because anyone who comes to him must believe that he exists and that he rewards those who earnestly seek him. (Hebrews 11:6)

> Trust in the LORD with all your heart and lean not on your own understanding; in all your ways acknowledge him, and he will make your paths straight. (Proverbs 3:5–6)

Of course, our confidence in God is based on His entire Word, so I challenge you to deepen your relationship with God by studying His Word. "In the beginning was the Word," says John 1:1, "and the Word was with God, and the Word was God." God speaks to you through the Word, and you strengthen your relationship with God through your understanding of it.

So the foundation of your authentic confidence is your faith, which is comprised of hope and certainty. Faith is your belief that God is with you and that He has your best interests at heart. You cannot see the whole picture, but God can—and in that you can be confident. If you dig deeper spiritually—through God's Word, prayer, and meditation—you'll hear God's promptings more easily.

Don't allow the enemy to fool you, though, when you don't hear anything. Sometimes we can get our answer by reading the Word. And sometimes we get our answer in the fact that God has said nothing. His silence may be a prompting to pause and persevere until you hear further instruction.

Your confidence soars when you believe truly believe God. Do not be afraid. Do not doubt. Just believe.

Confidence Prayer

Lead me onto the path of boldness, courage, and unwavering faith. Empower me to build my confidence through faith in You. Guide me to the scriptures that will address the specific areas in which I struggle with believing and trusting that You have great things in store for me. Help me fully understand and embrace faith-based confidence—that is, authentic confidence. I choose to trust You to hold me in securely in the palm of Your hand.

Confidence Journal

What are you afraid to hope for—for fear you might not get it? What action are you nevertheless willing to take toward this hope—and when will you take this step?

Confidence Builder

Today, identify and take a specific step toward your dream or goal. You can choose a baby step, such as verbalizing your hope and sharing it with someone. After all, "the tongue has the power of life and death" (Proverbs 18:21). If it's not possible to take action today, then take a look at your calendar and schedule a specific action on a specific date and time in the very near future. Don't let an opportunity to take the first step pass you by.

Day 9

Reject Lies

> I have three beliefs that I know are sabotaging me: (1) you can't be a Christian and be successful in corporate America, (2) you have to play by society's rules, not God's rules, in order to be successful, and (3) if you didn't complete your degree, you have little value.
>
> —Jasmine, 27

Briana was a thirty-one-year-old marketing manager with a strong drive to defy the odds of her upbringing and make it big financially. Despite earning $140,000 per year and living in a new home she'd purchased in a prized neighborhood (ironically close to the other side of the tracks where she grew up), she struggled between hanging on to the life she had created versus pursuing the life that called to her from within.

"Before I do what I really want to do, I've got to prove that I can succeed at a higher level than anyone would have ever imagined. I have to prove that a girl growing up poor can become wealthy. I want to have a rags-to-riches story," she insisted.

Seeing that she was fixated on money and how much of it she could make, I asked Briana who she would be with a regular job. "I wouldn't feel very important. I think people would look down on me the way they looked down on my family when I was growing up. I don't ever want to feel that way again," she explained. The wounds of feeling "less than" at any stage of life can impact your ability to see yourself realistically in the present.

As I probed deeper, Briana casually mentioned her mother's salary—$38,000 annually—when she was growing up in the 1980s and early 1990s.

"You consider $38,000 a year in 1990 poor?" I asked.

"Yeah, we really struggled," she said emphatically.

"I believe you may have struggled, but you do know that your mother's salary was above average at that time? In fact, that's probably about how much money my mother made when I was growing up—and we weren't poor!"

Briana grew quiet.

"Well, that would mess up my story," she said—only half joking.

Briana had a story in her mind: she grew up poor (rags), and now she was headed for financial abundance (riches). If she hadn't really been poor to begin with, she felt, her success would be less impressive.

Even more significant, though, is how she felt while growing up: deprived, poor. She felt that everything was a financial struggle. Even some family members had made comments that separated their upper-middle-class status from her mother's and her financial status.

Whatever had actually occurred, Briana felt less than. And that feeling continued to taunt her, serving as a driving force behind her desire to make increasingly more money even at the expense of her personal life.

Lies from the past that you believe and carry with you in the present can cause you to overcompensate and take an out-of-balance approach to life. In Briana's instance, the quest to feel significant led to an endless chasing after money. She bought into the lie that she inferred from the behavior of people around her, people who became the role models she looked to as an adult: money equals success. Never mind that this statement isn't true. If Briana believed it, it was true for her, and as long as others had more money than she did, she would lack confidence about her status, accomplishments, abilities, and worth.

The key for Briana was to move from equating money with success to believing the truth of God's Word. And it teaches that our success lies in living out God's will for our lives.

In our culture, we are constantly bombarded with images of what it means to be successful. Sometimes the images come from the outside world through various media, and unfortunately, at others times those false ideas come from the very people who should affirm and embrace us for who we are.

I challenge you to raise your awareness of the beliefs that are keeping you from fully being yourself. Some women, for example, have a long-held belief that being feminine means being demure and unassertive. As a result, they don't speak up and ask for what they want at work. Yet you must shift your belief to understand that being assertive is a positive trait, one that can used in a way that respects you and the person with whom you are communicating.

I coached one client on this sort of thing. Michelle had an MBA and more than fifteen years of experience in the business world when, a year and a half ago, she was laid off due to her company's downsizing. She decided to pursue an entrepreneurial dream, but she struggled every step of the way.

"I never have enough money, so I spend all of my energy trying to keep my head above water," she confessed. "I'm beginning to think that my problem is linked to my belief system. Deep down, I don't believe in my ability to be successful. How do people start believing something different about themselves?"

I congratulated Michelle on her success—because she had truly accomplished much—and affirmed that her observations about herself were keen. "It can be frustrating to try to succeed, only to realize that you're sabotaging your success with your beliefs about yourself," I told her.

In addition to negative beliefs, these five behaviors often sabotage success:

- lacking a plan
- not being specific about what you want
- burning bridges
- lacking focus and discipline
- not taking action

Since Michelle spent most of her energy trying to survive, she had less time to plan, focus, and take action on the crucial aspects of her business needed to succeed. It was an important step to become aware of the beliefs that paralyzed her progress and then change what she believed.

For example, if she believed she couldn't be successful, that belief could manifest itself in many ways: procrastinating on projects, allowing her fear of failure to keep her stuck in a rut, or unconsciously communicating her negative beliefs to clients and prospective clients. As a result, she would reinforce her negative beliefs by creating circumstances that supported those beliefs.

I encouraged Michelle to take out a piece of paper and list the reasons she didn't believe she could be successful. The results stunned her: many of the reasons she noted were based on experiences from the past, which didn't necessarily reflect what was true anymore. So I encouraged her to tackle that list and replace the negative beliefs with positive ones.

This was Michelle's new start. Even if she didn't feel comfortable doing so, I encouraged her to act her way to success and to take new actions to support her positive beliefs. As Michelle learned in this exercise, you too may never feel secure if your confidence is based on what you do, what you have, or who you know.

Notice the lies that you believe about yourself and your circumstances—and what those lies mean to you. An untrue belief only does damage because we interpret its meaning in a way that limits our ability to have authentic confidence as we act and interact.

Be honest with yourself for a minute: What lies do you believe about yourself and life that sabotage your confidence? Here are a few common ones:

- ☐ *Others will always be more or have more than I do.*
- ☐ *People with money are smarter, more worthy, or more successful.*
- ☐ *People without money are lazy, incompetent, or undeserving.*
- ☐ *Money equals success and self-worth.*
- ☐ *People who look like supermodels are happier, luckier, and better off.*
- ☐ *Other people have some special gift or knowledge that I don't have access to, and that explains why they are more successful.*
- ☐ *I don't deserve success.*
- ☐ *I'm not lovable or even likable, so people don't really want to be around me.*
- ☐ *In a romantic relationship, I must give up my identity to accommodate my mate's interests and goals.*
- ☐ *No one's interested in listening to what I have to say.*

- ☐ *Others are created for a unique purpose in life, but I'm not.*
- ☐ *I don't have what it takes to succeed in life.*
- ☐ *I am what I do for a living.*
- ☐ *I am what I make for a living.*
- ☐ For women only*: Assertiveness isn't feminine, so a woman shouldn't assert herself.*
- ☐ For men only: *To be a man means to know the answers.*
- ☐ *I'm not attractive unless I meet the media's standards of beauty.*
- ☐ *When someone else has more than I do, that means I get less.*

Are you surprised at the lies you believe?

Look again at the list, and remember this: if you believe that if others have more, you'll automatically have less, then authentic confidence will continually elude you. You'll not be able to celebrate others' successes, and you will live in fear whenever someone else appears to be getting ahead in life. That person's success is a threat to your success.

How can you be confident if you are constantly looking over your shoulder to see if anyone is gaining on you?

Dare yourself today to focus on God, not on others. Give yourself the challenge of putting your trust in God and His ability "to do exceedingly abundantly above all that [you] ask or think, according to the power that works in [you]" (Ephesians 3:20, NKJV).

Confidence Prayer

Thank You for challenging me to question any beliefs that don't reflect Your loving truth. Help me see these lies for what they are and resist the temptation to buy into them. Grant me the wisdom to replace lies with Your truth. Transform my thinking in the miraculous way that only You can.

Confidence Journal

What belief—what lie—most undermines your confidence? With what truth will you replace this belief?

Confidence Builder

Fast from media today. Turn off the television and the radio. Don't read magazines, the newspaper, online news, or gossip columns. Notice the difference in how you feel.

Day 10

Stop Keeping Up Appearances

> Television and the media flash these unrealistic images in front of us and tell us this is what we should look like, drive, have, etc. And we believe it!
>
> —Rachel, 42

Things can be a security blanket for those who feel insecure. Whether those things are accomplishments you can brag about, an expensive car, jewelry, a house, brand names, or even who you know—too many people are deep in bondage, holding on to a security blanket that inadequately shields them and keeps them from dealing with their deepest fears. External pressure is always there to try to convince you that you are not good enough. It presses you to believe that you need more of everything—more money, better looks, more education, and a better personality. Where does the external pressure come from in your life?

People you know, like family, friends, or acquaintances?

People you don't know?

You can embrace the pressure and even give it room to grow and loom larger. Or you can release it by refusing to give it a say in your life. When we feel our confidence waning, it is often because we have turned over the power to define ourselves. We've allowed someone or something else to tell us who we are and what makes us valuable and important. I want you to notice the aspects of your life that you see through the eyes of other people. How does this perspective make you feel? How does it impact your decisions and how you value your own needs and desires?

Denise found herself succumbing to an imagined external pressure about a major purchase she had made. She owned a luxury-class vehicle, which she had paid off a couple of years earlier. It was the least expensive model of a well-regarded European automaker, but that fact made her feel a bit self-conscious. She admits most people were probably not checking out the model of her vehicle, but in her mind, the whole world noticed that hers was the bottom of the line. Her authentic self felt very good about having been disciplined enough to pay it off early. She was using the money that was freed up from not having a car payment to build her savings and eliminate debt, an act that gave her confidence in her ability to be a good steward over her resources.

Among a group of friends she perceived as being more financially successful, Denise had begun to feel insecure about her car. In retrospect, she admits that no one had said or done anything to indicate disapproval of her car. "I don't think they looked down on me, but I allowed their material success to cause me to feel insecure because my success didn't appear to measure up to theirs," she said.

In essence, she viewed herself—wrongly—through the eyes of others. She put others on a pedestal, then stepped outside of herself, stood up on the pedestal with them, looked down with a wagging finger at herself, and proclaimed, "If you want to be up here with us, the price of admission is a fancier car."

The pressure of what she perceived others to think about her was intense. To alleviate the external pressure and the insecurity that originated from it, she sought an external remedy.

Denise bought a new and showier vehicle.

Was her decision aligned with her financial plans?

No. She ignored everything she knew in order to escape the pressure of imagined expectations. No one expected or verbally pressured her to purchase a new car. She created the expectation out of an insecurity that prompted her to value what she owned over who she was. As a result, the new car gave her a false sense of confidence. But the same insecurities that led her to buy the car were not alleviated by the presence of a nicer car.

What could Denise have done differently?

When she began to feel the pressure caused by these relationships, she could have been more truthful with herself and explored the insecurities as they arose: "I'm feeling less than. What's that all about? What behavior am I tempted to engage in when I feel this way? What behavior will empower me?" Honestly answering these kinds of questions for yourself—and then taking healthy, confident action based on your answers—requires courage. It is much easier to succumb to pressure and temptation. Living on the surface doesn't require honest reflection and spiritual growth. The problem is, the more you succumb to external pressure and temptation, the less confident you feel about who you are and your value as a person. Your confidence grows when you begin caring more about what you and God think about you than about what everyone else thinks. Your confidence grows when you focus inward.

The insecurities remained for Denise, and as she sought to alleviate them through more material status symbols, she finally decided to face the truth. "It wasn't about the things," she admits. "It was about what I perceived those things to mean. The truth I know now is that 'things' don't mean a thing." Denise identified and let go of that security blanket.

Authentic confidence comes from within. It has absolutely nothing to do with what you own, who you know, where you live, or what you drive. Authentic confidence is about knowing that you are here for a reason, that you have a unique ability to bless others, and that as long as you remain within God's will for your life, you will be successful. That's all that matters. I want you to know and embrace the truth that your confidence comes with knowing that God is with you. He created you and molded you to be who you are. He values you. He loves you. He has placed greatness within you. And your greatness doesn't look like anyone else's.

A test of my confidence comes every time I speak publicly, which is pretty often. I've consistently found my way through it by focusing inward, and I'll share an example. Speaking is something that comes naturally for me, yet doubts flash through my mind nearly every time I get ready to speak. As I stood in the wings of a convention center stage for a speaking engagement in Canada, irrational doubts ran through my mind: *There are twelve hundred women out there waiting and expecting you to tell them something new, something profound, something entertaining. That's a lot of women. Their expectations are high. Do you even remember what you were planning to say?*

As my thoughts began to spiral in a direction that was diminishing my confidence, I took a deep breath and focused my thoughts inward. *This is not about you, Valorie,* I reminded myself. *It's about God working through you. It doesn't even matter what you were planning to say. It matters that you be yourself so that you are an instrument of service. You sincerely want to see these women live more fulfilling lives. Speak from a place of love, and all else will fall into place.*

Instantly, I felt the pressure ease. I remembered all the previous engagements when my thoughts started aiming for an unhealthy direction and worry attempted to overcome me. In each and every instance I recalled, God enabled me to speak powerfully, purposefully, and lovingly. After I spoke, I'd received an outpouring of love and gratitude for the message I had shared.

Why is it that we forget the positive outcomes we've experienced and imagine all the negative possibilities that are highly unlikely to happen? I believe it's the enemy's way of distracting us from God's truth for our lives. If you're not intentional about focusing inward to regain control of your thoughts and embrace the truth, you will experience unnecessary worry that undermines your confidence. My speaking engagement that day in Canada, which included three main stage keynotes in one day, was the most powerful series I had delivered to date. I was in a state of flow. I delivered my words with confidence, ease, compassion, even humor.

And I learned an important lesson.

We should expect doubts to cross our minds when we are entering a situation that challenges or stretches us. Expect doubt. Expect insecurity to rear its ugly head. But have a plan of action prepared that will enable you to counter those obstacles with the truth.

Focus inward, and remember your own testimony. Remember that you are not doing it alone. God is with you. He's working through you. He's preparing you for something more. Rest in His strength. Listen for His encouragement. Embrace His peace. Don't rely solely on your own strength and strategies. Leverage divine strength and guidance with the gifts and talents you've been given, and you will be unstoppable.

Feelings are honest, but they are not necessarily the truth.

I first heard this statement from coaching pioneer Thomas Leonard, the late author of *The Portable Coach.* An aspect of focusing inward is noticing the lies that external pressure is often built upon. When the doubt that enters your mind is, *You're not good enough,* you must counter it. That statement simply isn't true. You are more than good enough. You don't have any more time to waste buying into lies about yourself, lies that sabotage your success. Make the decision to notice what you say to yourself that undermines your confidence.

Now, remember Denise?

When she realized that she could've asked herself and God the important questions before she bought the new, more impressive car, and then when she asked those questions in that moment, she easily spotted the lies her insecurity was based upon. She was feeling less than, but she was not less than. She finally came to the place of acknowledging that just because she felt less than didn't mean she needed to take an action that was based on that inaccurate feeling. The car couldn't make up for how she perceived herself. She had to peel back the layers of her insecurity to get to the core. The car was just a symptom of the external pressure she'd reacted to. She admitted feeling less than while simultaneously acknowledging that what she felt was not the truth.

You see, feelings are honest, but they're not necessarily the truth. What you feel is what you feel—and when you acknowledge those feelings, you're being honest with yourself. This is the first step to healing. Feelings help you see where you are emotionally. But the truth is about how God feels, how He sees you.

Aspire to live by the truth. Authentic confidence is based in truth; if you live by your feelings, you'll never experience authentic confidence.

The exhausting and elusive chase to be enough, have enough, and do enough to satiate our insecurity is a vicious cycle. It doesn't end unless you put a stop to it—and you have the power to make that choice.

Confidence Prayer

Sometimes the external pressure feels so strong, Lord. Take me under Your wing and help me rest in You. Matthew 6:33 says, "Seek first his kingdom and his righteousness, and all these things will be given to you as well." Help me remember this scripture when I lose confidence and find myself giving in to unrealistic expectations. Help me find my confidence in You.

Confidence Journal

What is the biggest pressure that persists in your life? When you succumb to this pressure, what void does it fill or insecurity does it meet?

Confidence Builder

Today, identify your security blanket—and leave it behind. Don't mention it or use it to comfort yourself when you feel insecure or unsure. Instead, just be who you are without it.

Day 11

Embrace Imperfection and Follow Passion

> Our culture encourages people to be superficial. We are really big on cleaning the outside of the bowl. If you saw someone cleaning the outside of a bowl and ignoring the dried food caked up on the inside, you would say that person is neurotic. Our culture attempts to regain control by overcontrolling meaningless and visible areas of our lives.
>
> —CRYSTAL, 46

In the midst of sharing a story with about four hundred women at a luncheon in Raleigh, North Carolina, I lost my train of thought. I mean, I completely forgot my point. I don't know what happened. I started a perfectly good sentence, but the rest of the sentence simply escaped me. I considered my options for a split second. *Should I fake it and just make something up?*

The problem was that I literally couldn't remember what point I was trying to make, so if I made something up, a bad situation could quickly get worse. So I stood there, frowned animatedly, and then gazed hopefully at the sharp businesswomen who had been listening intently to my story. "I gotta tell you somethin'," I said in an "I'm embarrassed but I know you'll understand" tone. "I'm not as young as I used to be, and I just totally lost my train of thought. What was I telling you?"

Some of the women looked as if they thought I was joking. Some of them laughed hysterically. And the rest of them, thank God, shouted out an answer to my question. With a little help from some women in my audience, I was quickly back on track.

What could have been a painful experience of pretending I hadn't forgotten what I was talking about and my audience then pretending they hadn't noticed became a humorous bonding experience for me and this group of women. I allowed myself to be fully human (hey, we forget things sometimes). Giving myself permission to not have to live up to an unattainable standard of perfection took the pressure off me to perform. When the individuals I was speaking to saw that I was comfortable being human, they connected more deeply with my message. During my book signing after the event, many of them specifically mentioned that they "loved it when I forgot what I was saying." Now, I didn't love forgetting, but I appreciated their appreciation of my humanness.

You can find great confidence in knowing that you don't have to be perfect to be effective. In fact, human beings aren't perfect. It's our nature to be imperfect. If you embrace your own imperfections, you can free up your energy to focus on serving others and making an impact rather then using your energy in trying to do everything right.

What could you do to relieve some pressure by giving in to your imperfections? Give one or two specific examples of imperfections and courses of action.

____

____

____

____

You can never be fully confident if your expectation is that you'll be perfect. That's an expectation you simply can't meet, and if you don't let go of that expectation, you will constantly be bracing for disappointment. It's impossible to be confident when your success depends on an unattainable standard. If you choose this route (and most of us have at some point in life), you'll find yourself regularly covering up imperfections so that they'll go unnoticed. Even if you believe you've covered the imperfect, you should never believe that others have bought into your cover-up. A spiritually discerning person will pick up on your ego and pride. Furthermore, the cover-up creates a barrier that hinders your ability to develop an authentic connection with the people around you.

If people can't trust you to be real, they'll wonder what else they can't trust you to be. Ultimately, this lack of authenticity impairs your ability to succeed.

Embrace the fact that you'll simply not know everything perfectly or be able to do everything perfectly—and that's okay. The sooner you get comfortable with the fact that you're imperfect, the sooner you'll manifest authentic confidence in your life.

Of course, embracing your imperfections does not mean neglecting the pursuit of excellence. "Whatever you do, work at it with all your heart, as working for the Lord, not for men," Colossians 3:23 advises us. It is essential that you balance doing your best with the inevitable imperfections that come from simply being human. There are times when God uses persistent mistakes and imperfections to steer us away from a particular path and toward another. If you find yourself consistently trying to do something for which you simply do not have an aptitude—or in some cases, a good attitude—ask God whether He's trying to show you something. There's no use attempting to be confident at something that's not the right fit for you. This principle can be true both personally and professionally.

"Delight yourself in the LORD and he will give you the desires of your heart," Psalm 37:4 says. When you discover and then pursue the desires of your heart, you tap into an element of your being that can fuel a level of confidence and enthusiasm that emanates from the core of who you are. Here's how:

Tap into your passion,
and you'll discover authentic confidence.

To free up some personal time and let go of chores I don't enjoy, I decided several months ago to treat myself to a regular housecleaner. As I typed at my desk one morning last week, Caroline entered my home office. Smiling, she busily moved big pieces of furniture so that she could vacuum and dust behind them. Caroline is a diligent entrepreneur who followed her passion and now enjoys a successful business doing what she loves. Her passion? Cleaning! Yes, cleaning.

As I observed the contented and confident look on her face while she fluffed pillows on a nearby sofa, it brought a smile to my face, and my curiosity was piqued. She was clearly in her element.

"Caroline, how did you get into this business?" I asked.

She smiled broadly and began to explain in her cheery Nigerian accent, "When I moved to this country in 1987, the only work I could get was as a nanny. It was so boring. The baby slept all day, and to keep myself from going stir-crazy, I started cleaning the house. I love to clean!" She nearly sang the words, "I love to clean!" Her kind of zeal comes only from a person who is doing work that taps into her gifts and brings her joy.

And Caroline's joy is my dread—that's the point. My passion may bore you to tears and vice versa, but that's what makes each of our passions so unique.

Caroline reinforced this idea, "The baby's mother was amazed at how thorough I was and started recommending me to her neighbors and friends," she explained. "By 1988, I had my own business, and it's been growing ever since."

Caroline's enthusiasm shines through both her cleaning efforts and willingness to learn. To increase her business, she even took up a third language (Spanish) a few years ago so that she could hire and converse with Spanish-speaking employees who wanted to work for her. Caroline and members of her team clean between seventy and eighty houses every week now.

When you do what you love, you give 110 percent, and that kind of effort attracts opportunity. When you do what you love, your confidence increases naturally and dramatically. But that energy won't even feel like something you'd call confidence. It's so much a part of who you are that you move forward knowing you're on the right path.

Confidence Prayer

Thank You for creating me just as You did, God, with all my imperfections and my passions. I trust You didn't make any mistakes. Help me simply be myself—passionately and completely. Where I have buried my passion, help me discover it again. When I'm tempted to pretend in order to appear perfect, give me the confidence to simply be human and to do my best in every situation. Psalm 37:4 tells me that if I delight myself in You, then You will give me the desires of my heart. What an incredible promise. Continue to place Your desires for me in my heart so that I can have full confidence that what I want and what You want for me are divinely aligned.

Confidence Journal

In what ways do I attempt to cover up my imperfections? How would it feel to be free from the pressure to be perfect? What passion is still untapped in my life?

Confidence Builder

Today, when you make a mistake, let it be. If you need help, ask for it. If an apology is in order, offer it promptly.

Day 12

Let Go of Comparisons

> I feel very inferior to others' accomplishments—or at least I used to. I'm learning to say, "Hey, this is my success. That is their success. One has nothing to do with the other."
>
> —Leila, 45

How do you feel when you compare yourself to others? It's a question I asked just over three hundred people in my confidence survey, and their answers covered a wide spectrum. Here are some of them.

A thirty-something professional, who is also the single mother of two, said, "When I see old friends who remind me that I was the 'most likely to succeed' and who have wonderful husbands and growing portfolios, I feel like a little girl with her nose pressed against the window of a beautiful candy shop where a wonderful celebration is going on, but I'm not allowed in. I know it's self-defeating, and the reality is that a lot of my friends who are married would trade places with me in a heartbeat. So I usually try not to stay there long, because it makes my emotions range from feeling sorry for myself to getting mad all over again at the lousy men I allowed in my past."

Another woman named Winifred said, "I rarely compare myself to others. But the times when I have gave me confidence to know if that person could accomplish whatever, then so could I."

Jackie told me, "I gain confidence from seeing others who've succeeded at something I want to accomplish."

Tim said, "Sometimes the comparisons are encouraging, and sometimes they are discouraging. In every case, they are inadequate for validating me. My real test is whether I am using the talents God gave me to see my true potential come to pass."

Kim said, "I sometimes compare myself physically to others because my body has changed since I had children. I remember what my body used to look like and how sexy I was before children. Now things have moved different places, and I am a little over thirty."

Do you notice the common threads? More than 79 percent of the respondents said that they sometimes compare themselves, their accomplishments, their looks, and their possessions to others. It's so tempting and so easy to look at other people's lives and feel that you somehow missed the boat: *Everyone else has it figured out. Why don't I?*

This way of thinking is just more bait that the enemy holds out to hook you into believing that you can't have what God means for you to have. When your perception of yourself is skewed, the grass doesn't merely look greener on the other side. It looks lush and thick while your little plot is a chunk of dry, cracked mud.

Boy, if we aren't careful, we can talk ourselves into a real depression. So, when things aren't going the way you'd hoped, be careful to keep your life in perspective. Be intentional about refusing to focus entirely on everything that's not right to you—and don't ever ignore your many blessings.

I was nineteen years old before I realized I could sing. I come from a musically gifted family. Some play multiple musical instruments by ear. One of my cousins sings opera. Another has written more than fifty songs. Others simply have amazing, anointed voices they use to lift up in praise in music ministries in their respective churches.

Music is central to our family. At any family gathering—Christmas, a reunion, a wedding—someone sits down at the piano to play, and the rest of us sing. Well, *some* of us just listen, really. Because of the sheer talent all around me, I never considered that my little singing ability was significant.

Then one afternoon, while my mom and I were driving up Highway 101 from Monterey on the way to a local Miss California preliminary, I began singing freely and loudly to a song that had just come on the radio.

"You know, you sing really well," my mother said.

I looked at her, unsure if she was serious. "Really?" I asked.

"Yeah," she said encouragingly. "I think you should try singing at your next pageant."

I'd been competing in pageants since I was thirteen, and *dancing* was always my talent. Never mind my observation that dancers had a more difficult time winning than singers. Everyone knows whether someone can sing or not, and most of us consider that ability a real talent. But dancing—and the talent it takes to do it well—isn't always as appreciated or as simple to judge.

So singing sounded like a very good alternative to my dancing.

I nervously contemplated the idea of singing on stage. To be quite frank, the thought seemed fraudulent at first. I mean, people don't just start singing when they're nineteen years old, do they?

Well, I did.

A couple of weeks later, I sang on stage for the first time, scared to death that someone was going to yell, "What are you doing up there singing? You're not a singer!"

In the minutes before I was to walk on stage, overwhelming anxiety rushed over me. *There are three hundred people out there. What on earth were you thinking when you came up with this idea?*

In a pageant-friendly gold lamé jumpsuit (it was 1992, okay?), I stepped onto the stage and belted out my song. I think my eyes were closed most of the time, but I made it through—my mother and my then-boyfriend (now my husband) cheering me on from the audience.

Over time, I took voice lessons and improved, but my nervousness was always there. I constantly fretted: *Will I remember my words? Will I hit all my notes?* These fears rarely came to mind when I was rehearsing, but they plagued me just before each performance. It wasn't until five years later, while competing at a Miss Texas preliminary, that I found my confidence builder.

Singing a 1939 jazz classic that had been remade by singer Vanessa Williams, I discovered the power of having a role model for confidence. Because I didn't see myself as a singer, I had difficulty imagining myself singing confidently on stage. So instead I imagined Vanessa onstage. I envisioned how she would stand, what she would think, and how she would connect with the audience. Then I imagined myself being like her—a successful, talented, beautiful performer—with an eager audience sitting on the edge of their seats.

This strategy has worked for me ever since that performance.

I went on to win a local preliminary and place third runner-up in my first and only attempt to become Miss Texas. To my surprise, I later learned that, in sixty-five years, I was only the second African American to make it to the top five. Not bad for a girl who still doesn't consider herself a singer.

So my strategy may seem simple, even silly, but it's practical, and it works—and it's a concept you can apply to a variety of situations in which you feel intimidated, afraid, nervous, or full of doubt. Picture someone you know would be fully confident, and then imagine yourself in that person's shoes for a moment. What would you feel?

Perhaps the intimidating situation is a conversation with someone you've avoided. Now is the time for you to confidently say what needs to be said.

Perhaps you're nervous about the salary increase it's time for you to receive or about another specific way in which it is time for you to step up to the plate, and you just cannot see yourself doing it. You are having a hard time imagining yourself taking the initiative that needs to be taken or succeeding if you do take the initiative.

See yourself in a new light by finding a confidence role model. A confidence role model can be someone you know, a historical person, or a well-known person. All that matters is that he or she inspires you to become more of who you already are. This person inspires you to rise to the next level in order to enjoy all that is within your reach.

My mother inspires me deeply. When she lost all her physical abilities after having a massive brain aneurysm in 2001, she went from being a vibrant, forty-nine-year-old career woman and mother of a third-grader (yes, she waited a couple of decades between children) to being unable to do anything whatsoever unassisted.

We fed her through a tube in her stomach because she had lost her ability to swallow. She had to be catheterized three to four times a day because her bladder wouldn't function. She couldn't stand up; when she arrived home after seven weeks in the hospital, we were overjoyed one afternoon when she was able to shuffle her feet two steps—and she could only do that if someone stood with her to ensure she wouldn't fall over. Few people could understand her speech, and her eyesight was severely impaired.

After a severe and potentially fatal setback at one point while she was in the hospital, a setback that meant days on a ventilator, she gained consciousness and was able to communicate with me. I leaned over the bed as I held her hand, and I placed my ear near her mouth.

In a weak voice, damaged by the intubation procedure, she whispered to me with slurred speech, "While I was lying there unable to breathe on my own, I kept thinking about Jesus. I imagined the pain He endured on the cross, and I told myself that if He could get through that, surely I can get through this."

Tears rolled down my face as I realized the depth of her faith and confidence in God. Jesus had become her role model of victory in the face of death.

Despite all the negatives she could have focused on, she focused on God's ability to bring her to a full recovery. And later, rather than compare her health to that of other people, she said on many occasions, "I have a condition that—with therapy—I can recover from. I'm grateful that if I had to go through a health problem, at least I know I'm not going to just keep getting worse. I've lost a lot, but I believe with God's mercy, I can gain it back."

She had full confidence—and still does—in her ability to fully recover. Only faith can generate that kind of confidence. Today, she has recovered between 80 and 90 percent of the abilities she originally lost.

In the area in which you find your confidence challenged, who could be your confidence role model? Keep in mind that your mentors do not necessarily have to be people you know. It's possible to have historical mentors or mentors you have come to know through books. Biblical mentors whose testimonies are shared in the Word also offer examples of how to live—and how *not* to live.

Consider a different person for each area of life in which you feel challenged, make notes, and then ask God to help you learn from what each role model offers you.

	CONFIDENCE CHALLENGE	CONFIDENCE ROLE MODEL
RELATIONSHIPS		
FINANCES		
HEALTH		
WORK		
SPIRITUAL LIFE		

Confidence Prayer

Lord, allow role models to cross my path who inspire me toward greater confidence in You. Free me from the temptation to compare myself with others—and infuse me with a level of confidence that allows me to celebrate and learn from the success of others. I choose today to honor the uniqueness of Your creation by never imitating anyone. Grant me the confidence to fully be myself while drawing strength from the manifestation of Your hand in the lives of those around me.

Confidence Journal

In the area that you find your confidence most challenged, who could become your confidence role model? Why have you chosen that person?

Confidence Builder

Use your confidence role model as a source of inspiration. Close your eyes and visualize yourself succeeding at heights you've previously only seen your role model achieve.

Day 13

Do Some Doubtbusting

> I usually *know* that I will succeed, *unless* the goal is to have a committed and compatible relationship.
>
> —Ellen, 52

As I type these words, I'm feeling quite nervous, and my stomach is upset. I know it's momentary, but the purpose of this experience must be for the wisdom I can learn from it and share with you. So I've decided to sit down at my laptop here in my lovely hotel room in downtown Chicago. I know there's no reason to be nervous, but this still happens sometimes when I'm about to speak. This morning my stomach is suffering because of the messages my thoughts are sending it.

I haven't thought literally about what I'm doing this morning—speaking to talented professionals for twenty-five minutes about a subject I've written and spoken about confidently and effectively on numerous occasions. The Lord sent me to these people. Of this I'm sure. Whenever I speak, I'm confident that God has a reason for my path crossing the paths of those who hear my message.

But in the moment, I can sometimes lose sight of this inner knowing. For a few minutes, the enemy's seeds of doubt breach my wall of confidence. I begin to focus on myself. That's where I am right now—focused on myself and on the person who invited me here. *Will that person be pleased with my talk? Will what I have to say be what these people need?*

So right now, as a vague cloud of doubt threatens to envelop me, I quietly call, "Lord, eliminate this doubt for me."

His answers immediately permeate my spirit. I take a deep breath and focus on why God opened this door. He must have something for me to share with these people. They are just people who have challenges, and I can give them a word that will help them push through those challenges and become more spiritually and emotionally mature in the process.

That's what I do. I inspire. I provoke thought. I am a vessel for God. The fear and doubt have melted. Yes, they have disappeared that quickly. I just needed a reminder to keep the doubts from spiraling out of control, as they were about to.

In Matthew 14, Peter stepped out in faith to draw nearer to Jesus when he believed he saw Him walking on the water. "Lord, if it's you," Peter said in Matthew 14:28, "tell me to come to you on the water."

Peter wasn't testing Jesus.

In fact, he was the only disciple on the boat to step out in faith or even call out to Jesus. The rest were afraid they were seeing a ghost.

When Jesus responded, "Come," Peter stepped out.

Most people hear God telling them to come—often in the form of a nudge in their spirit giving them direction—but too many of us look around, see the wind and waves, and never step out. Others are afraid that the voice they heard might not even be God's. Peter didn't think about what he was stepping into until he had already stepped into it! Then the reality of the situation hit him, and he took his eyes off Jesus. Only then did he notice he was standing on water, in the midst of waves and wind, and he began to sink. But Peter did one thing that we must all do when we begin to doubt: he called out to Jesus. And Jesus *immediately* reached out His hand and caught Peter.

Why do we allow doubt to spiral out of control when sometimes all we need to do is remind ourselves that God is with us wherever we go?

I believe it's because our thoughts are too vague to counter the seeds of doubt. We need to see our situation as something more than what it is. In my case, while sitting in my hotel room that morning before I was to speak, I reminded myself that I was just going to talk to some people about some things I love to talk about in order to help them become better equipped to achieve their vision. Literally, that's all there was to it. What's the absolute worst thing that could happen? Let's see… They could all fall asleep, boo me out of the room, or demand my honorarium be refunded. Sure, anything is possible. Have any of these things ever happened? No. Are any of these things likely to happen? No.

By being realistic about the situation, I was able to take myself from nervousness as I imagined the worst outcomes to a focus on the individuals who would be there and how I could help them.

In the moments when you feel most vulnerable to doubt—when the thoughts are spiraling and your nerves begin to tangle—stop yourself. Stand firmly on the *truth*. Remind yourself that God is using you and that He is with you wherever you go (see Joshua 1:9). Remind yourself that the situation is not about you. It's about what God is doing through you and what He is teaching you along your journey in preparation for something more. Also, we imagine that the world will come to an end if we don't do what we have to do perfectly. Relax.

"He who doubts is like a wave of the sea, blown and tossed by the wind. That man should not think he will receive anything from the Lord; he is a double-minded man, unstable in all he does" (James 1:6–8). This scripture uses *doubt* as a verb, which differentiates it from *doubt,* the noun.

When you are seeking to serve God, one of the enemy's strategies for throwing you off course is to use the people and circumstances around you to place seeds of doubt in your heart and mind. *Doubt* becomes a verb for you when you not only hear the enemy's lies but believe them and internalize them. When this happens, you become unstable in all that you do. You can have the skills but suddenly be unable to use them fully when the opportunity arises.

Have you ever seen this phenomenon happen to someone? A talented athlete or performer gets ready to perform at a crucial moment—and doubts creep in. The result can be painfully embarrassing.

Perhaps you've experienced this phenomenon yourself. If so, realize that the authentically successful person doesn't have room for doubt. There's no space to entertain it if you are to enjoy all that God intends for you. According to James, the double-mindedness that allows doubt to permeate one's thoughts creates instability. One moment, you're confident and believe in yourself; the next moment, you're nervous and doubting whether you should go for what you really want in life at all.

Some people believe they must know what is going to happen next in order feel stable and confident. Knowing means feeling confident. Many people base their confidence on knowing answers and being able to figure things out. I was well along in my spiritual walk before I realized that *not* knowing is okay. It can even be liberating, and that truth is counterintuitive. It seems only natural that confidence comes from knowing—and self-confidence *does* come from that. But authentic confidence trusts. It's nice to know, but knowing is not necessary.

We do not always control the thoughts that enter our minds, but we can control which ones we choose to dwell on. External factors—a distant memory, a conversation you hear in passing, or even something you see in a brief flash as you watch television—can take your mind in directions you had not even considered. Your job is to be aware as counterproductive thoughts enter your mind and to stand up against them. Doubt will show up like a door-to-door salesman on the doorstep of your mind. Send him away immediately. Don't open the door and don't listen to his sales pitch. Remind yourself who plants seeds of doubt and remember your power to destroy those seeds before they take root. That power can be found in James 4:7–8: "Resist the devil, and he will flee from you. Come near to God and he will come near to you."

Overcoming doubt is a challenge we each face, but take confidence in this promise from Scripture: God's Word calls us to be confident, believe His Word, and walk in His truth. That means you don't have to *feel* confident to *be* confident.

Confidence Prayer

God, in the first chapter of James You say that the person who doubts is like a wave of the sea, blown and tossed by the wind, and does not receive anything asked for from You. I don't want to be a doubter. Help me develop the habit of resisting the doubts when they are planted in my mind and immediately to focus my attention on You. I trust You, Lord, to save me from my own fears and hesitations and to fill me with the confidence that You are with me now and always. Thank You for transforming me day by day into a more confident believer.

Confidence Journal

In what way do you feel most vulnerable right now and most inclined to doubt God's ability to bring you through?

Confidence Builder

Today, take your eyes off the waves and the wind (doubts) and focus your eyes on Jesus (the positive possibilities).

Day 14

Speak the Right Body Language

> When I need a confidence boost, I throw my shoulders back and lift my head up! That's what my grandfather told me to do when I was a kid. It works.
>
> —STEPHANIE, 27

I was meeting with the production team for an event called THRiVE!—a live satellite broadcast to more than three hundred churches around North America. Serving as opening and closing speaker for the event as well as the emcee, I had a lot of responsibility. The day before the event, we were having a run through at Victory World Church in Atlanta, the location of the broadcast. The executive director of THRiVE! introduced me to the two main production managers, and we discussed some basic stage information I needed to know.

Then we headed to a side room where we sat down at a table to review the minute-by-minute rundown of the next day's onstage activities. The rundown had been sent to me weeks earlier, so I was familiar with it, but there were a few changes they wanted to review. As we wrapped up, I noticed that both producers looked a bit concerned.

Renee, the executive director, noticed too and zoomed in on the reason much more quickly than I ever would have. "Don't worry," she assured them. "Valorie is a very calm person. She understands the magnitude of what we're doing. She's just not going to get all worked up about it."

Immediately I saw relief on their faces.

I remember a time in my life when I would have been a nervous wreck about an event like that—and it would have showed. Twenty-five thousand women would be watching, and I would be speaking twice, interviewing two noteworthy individuals, and hosting the all-day broadcast. And I wouldn't be reading a Teleprompter. I'd be talking and glancing at notes occasionally. But a sense of complete peace enveloped me because I focused on God's abilities rather than my own. Women's lives would be enriched through this event whether I did my part perfectly or not; I truly was not in control.

Exuding a sense of calm in situations that could be stressful is a testimony to your faith and mine.

On Day 8, we said that confidence is based on faith and that to have faith you must trust and believe. I also shared that two more elements comprise authentic confidence: communication and preparation.

Communication is the outward manifestation of your faith, what you believe, whom you trust. Communication is more than what you say verbally, although the words that come out of your mouth are important. Communication is what you convey through verbal and nonverbal language. When you are not confident, what you say, however confidently, can be contradicted by your body language.

Today, let's focus on the keys to looking confident—and the body language that leaves you looking and feeling otherwise. Many psychologists contend that slumped shoulders and a low-hanging head are a fight-or-flight response brought on by low self-esteem.

Physiologist Walter Cannon first described this phenomenon, also called the acute stress response, in 1929. His theory is that an overall release of the sympathetic nervous system—which regulates such involuntary processes as heartbeat, breathing, and sweating—occurs when animals (including humans) react to fear or threats. When we are faced with danger, we have two options: face the threat (fight) or avoid the threat (flight).

How you feel affects how you position your body; hence the concept of body language has a foundation in science. Although we're rarely faced with the life-or-death dangers of ancient times, such as encounters with wild animals, our bodies still operate with a fight-or-flight response to perceived dangers. In other words, your fears prompt physiological responses.

What types of responses?

Consider this list that some psychologists point to as fight-or-flight responses in today's world, responses that make us look—or not look—confident. Notice how all of these responses are, on a physiological level, about protecting ourselves from the fear of what we perceive as a threat to our comfort zone.

- *Crossed arms:* On a basic fight-or-flight physiological level, crossing your arms is a natural response to fear that physically protects your body. It closes you off from attack or harm. Although you may cross your arms subconsciously, it conveys a message that you feel fear, and it sends a signal that you are not open to others, but rather need to be protected from them in some way. It's not a confident message.

- *Slumped shoulders:* Some psychologists suggest that your body naturally uses slumped shoulders to protect its vital organs. Again, it is a fight-or-flight response, the first movement that would bring your body into a tight ball should the pending fear turn out to be a real danger.
- *Raised shoulders:* The fear response of raised shoulders is a subconscious move that can protect one of the most vulnerable, most exposed parts of the body—your neck.
- *Tensed muscles:* Tensed muscles are a preparation response for the fight you anticipate based on the perceived threat that caused you to feel fearful. Again, this tensing up isn't conscious, but this subconscious body language communicates fear, the foundation of a lack of confidence.

So what types of body language communicate courageous, authentically confident responses to your environment? Practice the following behaviors, and you'll not only look more confident, but you'll also feel more confident:

- *Be still.* Maintaining a sense of calm even when there's turmoil around you conveys a sense of confidence. Avoid fidgeting and distracting movement. Ask someone you trust if you generally appear calm or nervous. Often, we don't notice our own fidgety habits.
- *Sustain eye contact with people.* Looking a person in the eye, and not looking away quickly, is a manifestation of confidence. Many people are uncomfortable holding eye contact for longer than one to two seconds, but looking someone in the eye for three to five seconds at a time says, "I'm listening to you. You're important. I've nothing to hide." Now this doesn't mean you should stare, but don't dart your eyes either. Practice sustained eye contact until it begins to feel comfortable.

- *Maintain good posture.* Slump your shoulders for a moment. Notice how you feel. I feel defeated, small, and more timid when my shoulders are rounded. How about you?

  Now roll your shoulders back and lift your head so that you're looking straight ahead. How does that feel? When you maintain good posture, you automatically *feel* and *look* more confident. Of course, some overdo it. There's a difference between puffing out your chest and having your nose in the air versus standing straight and tall. An exaggerated posture is a sign of trying to appear bigger than you really are—just as much a sign of low confidence as slumping your shoulders and trying to appear smaller.

  Square and direct is authentic. Although I've been unable to find specific research that connects good posture with the release of "confidence chemicals" in the body, I liken standing up straight with the feeling you get when you put a smile on your face. You can feel the endorphins racing to your brain, leaving you simply feeling better.
- *Keep your head straight.* Have you ever noticed how some people (maybe even you) cock their heads to the side when talking to someone? It doesn't convey confidence. Instead, the message it can convey is one of acquiescence or giving in. Certainly, there are times when this message is appropriate, but when you're trying to confidently communicate, it can be much more effective to keep your head straight.
- *Open your arms.* You'll very rarely see authentically confident people closing themselves off to others by crossing their arms, wringing their hands, or making small, closed gestures. An authentically confident person is open and welcoming. So while it may feel uncomfortable at times, keep your arms open, and your confidence will be part of your body language.

Certainly there are aspects of your appearance that can boost your confidence or diminish it. Authentic confidence necessitates an authentic appearance. In other words, you may look fabulous, but if your outward appearance does not resonate with who you truly are on the inside, you will not exude authentic confidence. So there is no cookie-cutter look that will give you confidence. Rather, you must delve deep to choose how you dress, how you style your hair, whether and how you wear makeup, and so forth. Just as discovering other elements about yourself, finding your own authentic look is a process. Enjoy it.

We're constantly bombarded with images of how we should look. I challenge you to let go of those images in favor of uncovering your authentic self. You are beautiful. You are wonderfully created in God's image. Make the most of what God has given you. And if there are any perceived flaws in your image, find a way for those flaws to contribute to your uniqueness, and glorify the Lord. Consider the beautiful words of Psalm 139:13–15:

> You created my inmost being;
>   you knit me together in my mother's womb.
> I praise you because I am fearfully and wonderfully made;
>   your works are wonderful,
>   I know that full well.
> My frame was not hidden from you
>   when I was made in the secret place.
> When I was woven together in the depths of the earth,
>   your eyes saw my unformed body.
> All the days ordained for me
>   were written in your book
>   before one of them came to be.

The Life Application Study Bible: New International Version expounds on these scriptures with this note:

> God's character goes into the creation of every person. When you feel worthless or even begin to hate yourself, remember that God's Spirit is ready and willing to work within you.... We should have as much respect for ourselves as our Maker has for us.

Because God made you, you are beautiful. Respect your body by taking care of it and by being excellent in your appearance. Look your best, not because of what others will think, but because it is an act of gratitude for the body with which you have been blessed. After all, "do you not know that your body is a temple of the Holy Spirit, who is in you, whom you have received from God? You are not your own; you were bought at a price. Therefore honor God with your body" (1 Corinthians 6:19–20). There are many ways for us to honor God with our bodies. One of them is to live healthfully. What you put on the inside will show on the outside. When what manifests on the outside is pleasing, you will feel more confident.

Looking confident is an important element of feeling—and actually being—confident. Just remember that looking confident from a place of authenticity is not about your looks as culture prescribes them. It is about the body language you manifest, the look you convey that most represents who you truly are, and the health you project based on how you treat your body.

Confidence Prayer

Lord, I understand that authentic confidence is projected from the inside out. As I grow in confidence, allow all that confidence to manifest in my body language.

Help me physically position and move my body in ways that trigger a mental feeling of courage, boldness, and authenticity.

Confidence Journal

What enhancement to your appearance would cause you to feel more confident? In what ways does your current body language project a lack of confidence? In what ways does your current body language project authentic confidence? Give examples of each. Now sit back and read what you've written. What patterns do you see? What are you learning?

Confidence Builder

Today, notice the ways you physically project both confidence and a lack of confidence. Review the chapter's descriptions of these physical manifestations of confidence, and then choose one of them to focus on today:

- Be still and calm in the midst of a hectic situation.
- Sustain eye contact with those with whom you are interacting.
- Maintain good posture.
- Keep your head straight.
- Open your arms.

Day 15

Prepare with Purpose

> I'm confident when I'm doing the things that allow me to live my purpose.
>
> —Gina, 35

After years of daydreaming about stepping out in faith, Kim found her courage. She left a six-figure salary in the Midwest to pursue her dream of becoming a singer-songwriter. She was sure God had told her to step out in faith—and she was obedient, arriving in Los Angeles just months after sensing the prompting of the Holy Spirit to do so.

In the process, she sought me as her coach. Kim was always fun to coach because her primary interest is personal and spiritual growth, so she was willing to stretch beyond her comfort zone. During one of her sessions, she shared one situation that caused her confidence to wane. As an aspiring entertainer, she was often asked to audition on the spot. As she described how this common practice sometimes threw her for a loop, I could feel her pain. Few people like performing on the spot.

I imagined myself in her shoes when I was an aspiring writer, having a publisher offer the potential opportunity of being published, and auditioning me by saying, "Look, we'll give you thirty minutes and a laptop. Write your best stuff, and we'll evaluate it on the spot."

The pressure and anxiety would be enormous. It was just what Kim was feeling. It wasn't that she didn't have the voice to impress and wow an audience. She knew that.

"So what is it that keeps you from being your best in those impromptu auditions?" I asked.

"I guess it's that I never know who I'm going to encounter and what type of song might work best for them. So I feel pressure to come up with the right song and sing it perfectly, all in a matter of seconds or minutes," she explained. "A lot of singers around here seem to revel in it, in part because their style is much showier than mine."

"I think I hear you saying that you don't feel prepared when you are asked to sing on the spot. Is that it, or is it something else?" I inquired.

"Yes! That's it. I don't feel prepared."

"So what would it take for you to feel fully prepared and ready to audition on a moment's notice?"

"Well, I think if I took some time to identify four or five songs that show my range and different aspects of my style and then I rehearsed those to perfection, I'd have the confidence I desire when I get those sorts of requests," she admitted.

So Kim made it her mission, over a two-week period, to choose and perfect her impromptu audition songs. In the first session after those two weeks had passed, I asked her how she felt about the possibility of facing an on-the-spot singing opportunity.

"I'm really ready now," she said. "I'm not nervous. I hope someone approaches me with that kind of request!"

One of the most common sources of a lack of confidence is a lack of preparation. When you prepare well for something, your confidence rises dramatically. Nervousness and anxious thoughts stem from the fear that you are not ready for the situation or opportunity that presents itself.

What are the keys to preparation?

- *Identify the core of your nervousness or anxiety about a situation.* Too often, we speak about our insecurities and concerns in vague terms. If you only scratch the surface of what you are nervous about, you'll never get to the root of the matter. It's the root of your lack of confidence that you want to get to so you can prepare in a way that makes a permanent change. For example, Kim first focused on the surface reason for her nervousness about impromptu auditions: her perception that other singers were showier, and her style has more of a laid-back, neo-soul, yet spiritual approach. That may have been true, but it was not the root cause of Kim's anxiety. Her style presented a unique challenge because it does not lend itself to the type of rousing singing that often grabs one's attention in a matter of seconds. She has a different kind of energy (think Sade meets CeCe Winans). She didn't want to be anything other than who she is, and yet if asked to join a band on stage for a song, she wanted to be able to confidently take advantage of the opportunity. She wasn't nervous about singing; she was confident in her abilities. Knowing that first impressions are most important, though, she was nervous about having to come up with something spontaneously that showcased her voice. Once she became clear about the source of her anxiety, she could identify a solution for relieving it. Think of each situation in which your confidence wanes. What's at the core of your nervousness and anxiety? Write down all the ideas that come to you. Then ask what's at the core of everything that comes to mind. What's the true issue?

- *Identify the action or circumstance that would alleviate the nervousness or anxiety.* Under what circumstances would you feel completely confident about this situation? The preparation process is about being intentional. It's about noticing what you need to both feel and be your best in every situation. I love the scripture in Proverbs that refers to things that are extremely small yet wise. It says, "The ants are a people not strong, yet they prepare their food in the summer" (30:25, NKJV). In other words, ants can go into the winter confident because they thought ahead and prepared accordingly. To prepare effectively, you have to identify what action you could take that would allow your confidence to increase, even skyrocket. Kim went from shrinking from opportunities and feeling anxious about going to certain events because she might be put on the spot, to seeking the chance to be in certain environments where she might be asked to sing without notice. It was a complete turnaround. The same can happen for you. In order to get around that challenge, Kim needed to be prepared in advance for the situation that might present itself at any moment. By preparing in advance, she had five songs of different tempos and genres that she loved to sing and that best showcased her voice (a cappella, if necessary). She was passionate about these songs—some that she'd written and others that were her own renditions of well-known hits.
- *Clarify what will need to happen in order for you to implement the actions you just identified.* Preparing can be easier said than done. If you keep that in mind, you will always ask yourself this question when you are making preparations that will build your confidence:

what needs to happen to clear the way for you to prepare? Preparation doesn't always take a great deal of time and energy, but it does take time and energy. My guess is that you already have a full day on most days, right? So how much time, energy, resources, and money will you need to prepare well? Identify what, if anything, you will need to do differently in order to carve out the time. For example, Kim had to be intentional about scheduling time to practice her songs. By scheduling the time, she made preparation a priority.

- *Take action.* Lastly, when you get clear about what you need to do, do it! It can be easy to get stuck in a rut of planning without actually taking action. Move forward in preparation, and your confidence will increase significantly.

Too many people stop moving forward when they feel unconfident. They take it as their lot in life rather than a challenge that can be overcome. It is imperative that you coach yourself to confidence by practicing self-curiosity—asking yourself the right questions and answering them truthfully. This process will empower you to quickly get to the root of your insecurity, hesitation, and doubt so that you can prepare in the way that will give you the most confidence.

Confidence Prayer

Thank You that with You all things are possible. Show me the best way to prepare for tasks that lie before me. Proverbs 20:18 says, "Make plans by seeking advice." I'm seeking Your advice, God, about the practical things I can do to prepare for the challenges and opportunities that are in Your plan for my life. I trust You will show me clearly, and I thank You in advance for Your faithfulness and love for me.

Confidence Journal

What do you feel God leading you to do to prepare in a way that will strengthen your confidence?

Confidence Builder

Today, identify a specific act of preparation that will build your confidence—and then do it. Remind yourself with each act that preparation is the antidote to doubt and anxiety.

Day 16

Speak Up for Yourself

> It's a defeated feeling to walk away from a conversation seething over what you should have said.
>
> —Jo, 41

Olivia is a sweet, smart, and otherwise savvy forty-year-old woman. Yet for some reason, she couldn't muster the confidence to tell the truth to an energy-draining, self-centered friend she has known since high school.

"It's important to me to be a good friend, and part of being a good friend is being nice," she said, adding, "I don't want to hurt her feelings. Sometimes that means telling a little white lie."

"And where in Scripture are we asked to be nice?" I asked. Olivia looked perplexed, as though this was a ridiculous question. "Of course God wants us to be nice," the expression on her face reasoned.

"Kind, yes. Truthful, yes. But nice?" I continued. "And please show me,"

I requested with an empathetic smile, "where it says that little lies are okay with God, but just not the big ones."

The frustrated but stubborn look on Olivia's face told me she understood my point but was steeped in her beliefs about what it means to be a good friend. By her definition, a friend can continually (for years) burden you with her problems without showing much concern for the challenges you might be facing. A friend can expect help while rarely giving it. And a friend can even make remarks ("You're not married, so you don't have anything else to do") that are insulting because she has apparently earned this right after being a friend for two decades.

I admired Olivia's loyalty, but it was tainted with some beliefs that were not serving her well. At its core, her dilemma was about mustering up the courage to have a difficult conversation and having the confidence to ask for and expect a mutually beneficial friendship.

One of the most common places where people lose confidence is in conversation. You can be confident in your mind, imagining yourself speaking the truth in a spirit of love, but when you are face to face, your confidence dwindles, and your vision of speaking your mind disappears. Have you ever had this experience? Sometimes it happens because we do not want to hurt people we care about, but more often than not, it happens because we have not given ourselves permission to set healthier boundaries, ask for what we want, and request the same respect we are willing to give. Consider these three approaches to returning an item to a clothing store:

- *Timid:* "I just wanted to know if I could return this?"
- *Assertive:* "When I got home with this sweater, I noticed that the zipper doesn't work, and I would like to get a refund."
- *Aggressive:* "I don't care what your refund policy is! You'd better give me a refund, or I'm taking this all the way to the CEO of this company!"

Note that the aggressive approach might get you what you requested. However, it will unnecessarily put salespeople on the defensive, perhaps even causing them to go out of their way to *not* meet your request. Second, it is a horrible way to serve as an ambassador for Christ in a world filled with rude, aggressive people who are entirely focused on *me, me, me!*

In order to speak with authentic confidence, which means speaking truthfully yet lovingly, remember these important points:

- *Be direct—both with your body language and your choice of words.* Don't say "uh" when you communicate. It conveys uncertainty and a lack of confidence about either yourself or the information you are communicating. Keep your head straight rather than tilting it to the side. Say exactly what you need to say without beating around the bush, repeating yourself, or rattling on. Adding extraneous information and sentences will dilute your message.
- *Speak slowly.* Pause if necessary. Think of the most successful people you know or admire. They probably do not rush when they speak. Powerful, confident people speak with authority. And when you speak with authority, you don't have to rush. Pause between important points you are making so that the listener can process the information and you can calmly gather your thoughts.
- *Speak in key messages.* As a former public relations professional, I'm always thinking in terms of key messages. When you communicate, know your key points. Communicate those succinctly. Too many details can weaken the impact of what you're saying. Of course, you can answer questions and give details if you are asked, but there is no need to begin a conversation with rambling stories and detailed explanations. Be confident and get to the point.

When you are succinct, you'll notice that people will respect how you have communicated with them even if they don't like what you've communicated.

- *If you haven't thought through what you want to say, don't speak for the sake of speaking.* When you are in an important situation, it is often better to say you'll be ready to speak about it at another time than to talk for the sake of talking. Proverbs 17:28 says, "Even a fool is thought wise if he keeps silent, and discerning if he holds his tongue."

As you consider conversations in which you want to speak confidently, consider this situation a friend found herself facing. She had told me that setting and communicating boundaries with needy family members was becoming increasingly important. Her family always seemed in need of money or baby-sitting, yet they never repaid the favors, let alone the cash. "One family member continues to abuse his health with habits and addictions that cause him to become ill and dependent on others," she said. "This has taken a toll on me personally. I feel used up and weary. I don't want this to affect my marriage. Thus far, my husband has stayed supportive and empathetic, but he wants me to take a stronger stand and say no to any more requests. I'm trying to do that, but I deal with so much guilt because this is my family. I want to honor my values by not turning my back on them."

Whether you're facing a similar situation or your boundary issues are with your friends, an employer, or someone you love, this truth applies: the sooner you make a decision to set boundaries, the sooner you'll experience less stress. Otherwise, you've allowed and even trained the person involved to use you and take you for granted. Not only does that behavior hurt you, but it also hurts them. They don't have to find their own solutions or be totally responsible for their problems because you're their crutch, and they can use the crutch whenever they want.

It's in this sort of situation that you must dig deep and ask, "What am I getting out of this?"

You know you love your family (or friends or job). But if you don't take care of your cousin's son this weekend, it doesn't mean you don't love your family. If you choose to use your money for you and your husband's goals and needs rather than digging them out of a hole repeatedly, it doesn't mean you don't love your family. Setting and keeping your boundaries means making a shift in how you define love.

Of course you will be there for your family in times of crisis, and you'll spend time with them, but don't let anyone manipulate you into feeling guilty because you don't give in to every request they make. Be kind and loving, but firm about the need to prioritize your time and resources.

Make a list of your new boundaries or rules for such situations—what you'll do in which situations as well as what you won't do. Also list the circumstances you won't take on from others. Here are the boundaries we worked out for my friend:

- I only baby-sit once per month and then only if I feel like it. It's my choice not to have children, but not having children does not obligate me to spend my time taking care of others' children.
- I don't allow others to dictate how I spend my time.
- I don't loan money to anyone unless my husband and I agree and feel led to give it—and if we loan money, we set out the terms clearly and in advance.

Be willing to say no. Even though you may feel guilty at first, do it anyway. Saying no to requests that take you away from your purpose, goals, and time with those you love will give you the room to say yes to your true priorities. You only have so much time, and you must use it purposefully.

In order to speak with confidence, you've got to be clear about who you are and what your boundaries are with the people in your life. Then communicate those boundaries directly and lovingly.

Confidence Prayer

God, I know Your desire is for me to speak the truth in a spirit of love. Proverbs 18:21 says, "The tongue has the power of life and death," and I want to speak life into every situation that is around me. Help me communicate clearly, succinctly, and confidently with those I know as well as those I don't. When I feel tongue-tied, speak for me. When I'm afraid to speak truthfully, give me courage. Help me speak up for myself as well as for others. And help me do so consistently and effectively.

Confidence Journal

In what ways could you improve your communication skills so that you will be able to speak more confidently in every situation? What are you willing to do now?

Confidence Builder

Today, when you speak, don't rush through your words. Instead, pause when you are saying something particularly important, and allow a sense of calm to permeate your words.

Day 17

Practice the Power of a Pause

> When I begin to head down the road of doubt or start speaking negatively about myself, I try to remember to take a deep breath and just stop it.
>
> —Chris, 33

It's so reassuring to know that even the apostle Paul struggled with doing the right thing. "I do not understand what I do," he wrote in Romans 7:15. "For what I want to do I do not do, but what I hate I do."

There is a simple habit that will empower you to overcome the temptation to shrink from authentic confidence—your true state of being—in favor of old habits not based in confidence.

You may think this change is about willpower, but the real issue is mastering your ability to take control of your thoughts at the very moment when temptation to not be confident feels strongest. That ability comes when we don't rush; a confident person isn't hasty. I call it harnessing the power of a pause. There are many moments when the power of a pause can transform the course of your day and even, over time, the direction of your life—because what you do daily creates the circumstances of your life. And pausing to make the right choice feels good, especially when instant gratification is staring you in the face!

Five simple steps can harness the power of a pause in your life. Harness the power of a pause to make meaningful changes when you are tempted to let old habits rule.

1. *Notice the temptation to act impulsively.* Be aware that the temptation is there, but do not allow it to take over. Expect it, then do something different—immediately. You may have to speak out loud to encourage yourself. Life and death is in the power of the tongue, so use your words to give life to your true goals. First Corinthians 10:13 says, "No temptation has seized you except what is common to man. And God is faithful; he will not let you be tempted beyond what you can bear. But when you are tempted, he will also provide a way out so that you can stand up under it."
2. *Pause and take a deep breath.* Breathing deeply can help you feel centered. When you are calm and steady inside, you connect spiritually and tune in to what really matters to you. Use your breath to slow yourself down so that you can be intentional about your choices.
3. *Ask yourself, "What action would move me closer to my true goal right now?"* Once you've noticed the temptation and taken a deep breath, ask this question that will empower you to choose the best thing to do.
4. *Ask for divine strength.* One of the reasons we get stuck repeating habits that do not serve us well is that we try to make changes in our own strength. But "the one who is in you is greater than the

one who is in the world" (1 John 4:4). That power within you is stronger than any other. Invite the Holy Spirit to give you in the moment the strength you need to take the best action. The strength not to overeat or be late or incessantly surf the Internet may seem like a silly or insignificant thing to pray for. Always remember, though, God cares about the little things you struggle with because the little things ultimately affect the bigger picture of your life.

5. *Repeat these steps as often as is necessary.* Our days are made up of moments, and there are plenty of moments in every day when we are tempted to do things that will take us off course. So repeat these four steps as often as you need to until the choices you want to make become habit. The more you resist the temptation and do something different, the more you build up the muscles to persevere on your path.

This process is especially important to master if you struggle with confidence in the area of finances or weight loss—two areas that can spiral out of control due to impulsive choices.

One of my clients recently reminded me of this fact. Michelle told how she'd accumulated more than sixty thousand dollars in student loans attending a private university to earn her bachelor's and master's degrees and to start (but never finish) law school. She didn't feel confidence about being able to work out a plan to pay off her debt, and her circumstances were compounding her doubts and insecurities.

"Although I know I'm drowning in debt, I can't seem to stop shopping," she admitted. "I have expensive taste and feel like I deserve to have nice clothes and a German car. I want to stop shopping, but my need to look good seems to take over every time I try to control my spending—and I simply whip out my credit card to pay for purchases. I quit even adding up my credit card balances. I think, all together, I probably owe more than twenty thousand dollars in credit card debt! With my sixty-thousand-dollar salary, I'll never get out of this hole."

Acknowledging her shopping and debt problem and then asking for help were wonderful first steps for Michelle. It's extremely stressful to shoulder massive debt. So here are four steps Michelle and I worked out to help her get rid of that stress as well as her debt—and these steps can work for you too:

1. *Face the truth about your money.* Most people who are in debt can't tell you exactly how much they owe. This is primarily because the total amount is overwhelming, so they'd rather not know. Today, add up what you owe on your credit cards, unpaid student loans, and any other outstanding balances. Also add up the total amount of interest you pay each month on the debt. (On eighty thousand dollars this may be as much as seven hundred per month or more, depending on interest rates.) Rather than beating yourself up about what you've spent, use this information as the starting point for a debt-elimination plan.
2. *Stop using your credit cards.* This may mean you need to cut them up and only use your debit card, or perhaps you can trust yourself to leave them in a drawer at home rather than in your wallet. Do whatever is necessary to put away the credit cards for good. Little purchases add up quickly! Harness the power of a pause to nip in the bud those impulsive purchases.
3. *Assess your income potential.* Find out how much your experience, education, and talents are worth in the marketplace. Then make decisions that will help you maximize your income. Whether that means pursuing better opportunities with your current employer, looking for a higher-paying position, or generating additional

income through a part-time business or job, do whatever is necessary to increase your income so that you can accelerate payments on your debt. Your confidence increases when you do not settle for making less than you are worth!

4. *Address the underlying issues.* Do you shop when you are feeling down? Do you get a high from shopping? What void does shopping fill for you? Consider making important behavioral changes. For instance, don't shop alone. Always shop with a list. And don't window shop. Only shop when and where you've planned and budgeted to do so.

These steps, especially employing the power of a pause, are helping Michelle turn around her present—and her future.

Michelle is not alone in needing this simple reminder to stop and change course when it comes to her finances. When asked, "In what area of life do you feel least confident?" 49 percent of the 310 respondents to my confidence survey said they felt *least* confident in the area of finances.

Our times don't help. We live in a world that moves fast and both enables and rewards consumption. It's easy to spend time and money fast and quick. So there's a bigger issue at stake when we speak of the power of a pause. When you implement the power of a pause, you are both exercising the discipline needed to make better decisions and being a better steward of the resources you've been given, which we'll discuss more in the upcoming chapter on how to make wise decisions. A person who consistently makes sound decisions is a confident person. She's a person who can trust herself to do the best thing at any given moment in time.

Those who are hasty or do not take the time to listen for the voice of the Holy Spirit often lack confidence in themselves because, during those key turning points in life, they have too often missed their signal.

Be confident enough to ask for divine guidance, then be willing to listen for your answer. Sometimes the most important action step is not moving forward, but being still and exercising discipline.

Confidence Prayer

Galatians 5:23 tells me that one of the fruits of the Spirit is self-control. Help me practice discipline and self-control so that in the moment I'm tempted to veer off track, I'll pause and intentionally get back on track.

Confidence Journal

What goes through your mind in the moment before you take an action contrary to what you really want to do? If you paused in that moment, what question would most effectively prompt you to make a better choice?

Confidence Builder

Pause when you feel tempted to do something that will take you off track. Ask for divine strength. Do the thing you really want to do even though another path would be easier. The long-term reward will be worth it! Write the following five steps on a sticky note or print them out and post them as reminder:

1. Notice the temptation.
2. Pause and take a deep breath.
3. Ask, "What action would move me closer to my true goal right now?"
4. Ask for divine strength.
5. Repeat these steps as often as necessary!

Day 18

Eliminate Confidence Stealers

> The voice inside me reminds me that I have made it through trials and tribulations, but sometimes the voice inside cannot be heard because of giant voices of doubt coming in to steal my confidence. Fortunately, the voices of my friends often outshout the echoes of doubt.
>
> —CARLA, 31

One afternoon in 1997, a couple of months after launching a public relations agency, I stood barefoot in my kitchen while a nurse extended his measuring tape to record my height as a part of an exam for new health insurance.

"Five feet one and a half inches tall," he said and began to move on to the next item on his checklist.

"Wait a minute," I said. "I'm taller than that. Will you measure me one more time to make sure?"

"Sure," he said, then measured again. "Yep! Five feet one and a half inches tall!"

I hadn't grown since tenth grade and had decided around that time that I should be taller. I had hoped and wished I would grow as a teenager because I was modeling a little bit and would have passionately pursued a modeling career if I had been tall. Of course, saying that I was five foot three (which is what I had begun doing around 1988) wasn't anywhere near being the five foot eight minimum I'd need for a modeling career, but that hadn't mattered. I'd said I was five foot three for so long that I didn't know how tall I actually was. Whenever someone challenged me about being five foot three, I quipped, "Don't you think I know how tall I am?"

As I stood in my kitchen that day with the nurse and his measuring tape, I reasoned that the measuring tape must be incorrect. It wasn't until a year later, when my company changed insurance companies once more and a different nurse came to my home, measured me, and said, "Five feet one and a half inches," that I faced reality.

Why was I so insecure about my height?

I was insecure because of how I interpreted it.

The meaning you assign to the facts of your life is what causes you to feel confident or secure. At one point in my life, being just over five feet tall meant being insufficient and disqualified from something I wanted. Because of my height I was disqualified from a fashion career and from becoming a pilot.

Of course, God creates us just the way He does for a reason.

Neither of those careers was meant to be my path in life. If I'd been tall enough, those would have been my choices. So, after the measurement a year later, I decided to change how I interpreted my height. I embraced it—and I even corrected my height on my driver's license.

Whenever we interpret things—whether it's someone's reaction to us or a perceived failure—in a way that doesn't serve us well, we can lose confidence. Embracing what actually is and trusting that it is that way for a divinely ordained reason can free you to have confidence in both who you are and where you are in life. There are all sorts of issues and challenges that can steal your confidence. Some of them—like convincing yourself that you are taller than you really are—may seem silly, but they are nonetheless real. All confidence stealers can be categorized as one of four culprits:

1. fear
2. doubt
3. insecurity
4. low self-esteem

If you allow them, these bad guys will constant chip away at your confidence. Sometimes all of them are at work simultaneously, and sometimes there is just one to contend with. Yet they are intertwined and often feed on one another. Fear is at the core of doubt and insecurity. Our fear-based thoughts are focused on the possibility of a negative outcome and the consequences of failure. Notice how these four themes may present themselves in your life.

To help you do so, I've identified seven confidence stealers that when present will almost always sap your confidence. No matter what area you're working on to build your confidence, if even one of these seven issues is present, your confidence will suffer. Preparation is the foundation in overcoming each of these confidence stealers.

If you need to, scan Day 15 to recall the importance of preparation, how it is an essential element of confidence and how the lack of it leaves you feeling unsure and anxious. If preparation seems like an unrelated topic, remember that worship and Bible study are preparation. Previous experience is preparation. Study and observation of success models is preparation. And so on.

- *Lack of knowledge.* "My people are destroyed from lack of knowledge," Hosea 4:6 says. A lack of the knowledge of God can be destructive to one's life. A lack of knowledge about how to accomplish the things God has placed on your heart can destroy your confidence. Whether in a relationship or on the job, many people lack confidence because they do not have the knowledge to experience success at the next level—and some of these people don't even realize it. Rather than seek out knowledge, they simply remain at the level where they are comfortable. And we human beings are comfortable when we know what's coming next. Fear of the unknown is one of the greatest fears that keeps people from moving toward their truest desires. On the other end of the spectrum are those who boldly and enthusiastically proceed toward a goal without the knowledge they need to succeed, overestimating their abilities. "It is not good to have zeal without knowledge, nor to be hasty and miss the way," Proverbs 19:2 says.
- *Lack of support.* In the confidence survey I took, many people reported that they lack confidence because they fear they do not have the resources to succeed. When you don't feel supported, your confidence wanes. So identify what makes you feel supported, and then do what you need to in order to drum up that support. "For lack of guidance a nation falls, but many advisers make victory sure," Proverbs 11:14 says. The New King James translation says, "When there is no counsel, the people fall; but in the multitude of counselors there is safety." This scripture teaches us that success is a team effort. When you are supported properly, you will succeed.

- *Lack of past successes (history, previous wins).* Past failures are one of the biggest causes of fear and a lack of confidence. But failures are not the only culprit. Having no track record of success can shake your confidence as well. It's important to build up your confidence by building on progressively larger successes. Be willing to start small and build a history of success for yourself. As you succeed at gradually bigger levels, your confidence will grow.
- *Lack of truth.* Whether you're deceiving yourself or being deceived by others, a lack of truth leads to a lack of confidence. You cannot feel good about yourself when you avoid facing the truth about yourself. Make a decision to practice self-curiosity when you are tempted to deceive yourself. In my book *What's Really Holding You Back?* I explain how your negative emotions send you messages if you are willing to listen for them. When you face the truth about yourself, God can show you your way in life. Being honest about yourself takes courage, but it will be well worth the effort as you accelerate the pace of your growing confidence and your success.
- *Influence imbalance.* Constantly concerning yourself with what others think diminishes the importance of what you think about what's going on in your own life. It is certainly okay to solicit opinions and insight when making a decision, but it is not okay to give greater weight to others' thoughts than you give to your own and God's guiding voice. There can also be an imbalance of influence when you are self-centered. Make sure that you are not so focused on yourself that you forget God is in this too. Focus on God's plan and direction for you.
- *Lack of relevant role models.* Seeing someone else accomplish what you seek to accomplish can be one of the biggest confidence boosters. This is why it is so common for children of successful

people to become successful themselves. Likewise, it can be such a struggle for people who have had few positive role models to succeed at a level higher than anyone who was in their environment. Success is possible, but those individuals will have to be very intentional about finding role models to help them see their own possibilities. If you are struggling in your marriage, you will gain confidence by seeing couples who struggled and overcame challenges. If you lack confidence that you can be a healthy weight, you will be helped by seeing others who have already lost as much or more weight than you seek to lose. Identify a relevant role model who will inspire you and give you confidence. "Listen to advice and accept instruction, and in the end you will be wise," Proverbs 19:20 says.

- *Unrealistic or unwise plan.* A plan that does not realistically connect the dots between where you are and where you want to go will diminish your confidence. You may attempt to convince yourself that the plan will work, but if in your spirit you doubt the plan, that weak plan will be a major confidence stealer.

So what can you do to protect yourself from these confidence stealers? Get knowledge. We began the list of confidence stealers with "lack of knowledge" because if you get knowledge and wisdom, you will automatically eliminate the other six confidence stealers. "Choose my instruction instead of silver, knowledge rather than choice gold, for wisdom is more precious than rubies, and nothing you desire can compare with her," Proverbs 8:10–11 advises. Building confidence is all about preparation, and the first step to preparation is knowledge. It's important to identify what you don't know, but need to know. So seek knowledge passionately, always learning and always growing. A thirst for knowledge builds confidence. It is therefore essential for you to ask yourself, *What knowledge would give me confidence?* For example, if you lack the confidence to ask for what you want, the missing 'knowledge' could be how-to information about negotiating or having difficult conversations. If you lack confidence in your ability to buy your own home or begin investing, knowledge will increase your confidence by decreasing your fear of the unknown.

So how do you get this knowledge you need? You can get it through experience, formal education, training, counseling, coaching, books, and observing and conversing with those who have been successful at the very thing you desire. Knowledge empowers you to get understanding and ultimately wisdom about how to make bold and confident decisions. As you increase your knowledge and then your understanding, you will dramatically increase your confidence.

Confidence Prayer

Lord, You know the things that diminish my confidence. Help me identify and eliminate each and every one of them. Give me the confidence to face things I may feel afraid to face.

Confidence Journal

What steals your confidence most significantly? What could you do to eliminate that confidence stealer from your life? When will you take that step? Answer these questions even if your thoughts are sketchy.

Confidence Builder

Today, take action on the issue you identified in today's entry in your confidence journal.

Day 19

Finish What You Start

> I think it's not only important to start with confidence, but to finish with confidence. I notice that in the beginning and toward the ends of projects is when my confidence is attacked.
>
> —JACQUELINE, 22

In responses from the diverse group of people I've surveyed and spoken to about the topic of confidence, I've been amazed to discover that one of the most common concerns that surface for many is, "Will I actually be able to finish what I set out to do?" or "Will I run out of steam before crossing the finish line?"

I say it amazed me because, although I have experienced a variety of doubts when I have contemplated particular goals in my life, the question of whether I'd finish what I start has never been one of them. I began to dig deep to determine why and to ask others who don't have this fear why they feel the way they do. As I searched for my answers and talked with others, some fundamental truths came forth.

Many people lack the confidence to begin something because they don't trust themselves to finish. Others have stopped dreaming altogether because they don't even trust themselves to get started with something new.

Persevering to the end is a decision that you make. It may take more sacrifice than you originally anticipated, but once you make a decision to move forward, you must be committed to sticking with it until the job is done.

So commitment is at the core. If you commit, the favor of God will be upon you. "Commit to the LORD whatever you do, and your plans will succeed," Proverbs 16:3 says. Commitment is about your word. You must establish as your standard that you always finish what you start. That makes your word trustworthy. And trust is an essential value for those who follow through on their plans. They want to be trusted.

"If a person can trust you," these people note, "he or she will respect you."

That respect must be earned. You can respect yourself if you can trust yourself to do what you say you are going to do. It is more important to your confidence that you can trust and respect yourself than it is that anyone else trusts or respects you. If you can trust and respect yourself, the trust and respect of others will follow. The reputation you develop as a result will boost your confidence, reinforcing your drive to follow through. Proverbs 22:1 promises, "A good name is more desirable than great riches."

Self-efficacy plays a central role in developing that reputation. I think of self-efficacy as a belief in one's ability to effectively control specific events in life. People with self-efficacy have confidence that they can do what they set out to do because they understand the power of focusing on the task before them until it is complete.

People who follow through were often taught as children that you always follow through. If you won't follow through, don't even start. This belief is deeply ingrained in those who consistently follow through. If you make a decision to become the kind of person who follows through on your word and your actions, you will grow in confidence as you build evidence of your ability to trust yourself.

I'll never forget the reaction of one of my friends when I completed my first book. I had told Lynn I was writing my first book and planned to self-publish it. I was very clear about that. A couple of days after the book came off the presses, I gave her a copy. She was perplexed.

"You wrote a book! Oh my goodness! I can't believe it!" she exclaimed as if she had had no idea of my plans.

I said, "I told you a couple of months ago I was writing a book."

"I know," Lynn admitted, "but people say that all the time."

In other words, she heard what I had said, but figured that "writing a book" could mean, "Maybe I'll finish in five years."

Chloe is a smart, streetwise, hard-working single woman in her thirties who wasn't satisfied with her below-average salary. She had a sizable sum of money in savings, though, and a strong desire to invest that money in a way that would lead her to financial freedom in her forties. Her desired investment vehicle was real estate, but the abundance of choices and options sometimes left her feeling overwhelmed and unqualified to make decisions. She discounted the knowledge she'd learned growing up with parents who were investors themselves and had shared lessons with her. She sometimes discounted her own intuition, research, and intelligence. She was diligent and thorough with every deal she considered, yet she found herself paralyzed and unable to make a decision when it was time to move forward. She lacked confidence in her ability to succeed in pursuing the passion that excited her most. She sought advice from people she perceived as knowing more. Sometimes she gave up her power to them and, in return, spent significant sums of money for their guidance on transactions that turned out to be fruitless.

"From my perspective, it seems that you don't trust yourself to make the best decisions for you. Do you think that's true?" I asked her.

"Absolutely it's true. I'm just so scared that I'm going to blow it, that I'm going to lose the money. I just don't have confidence in my ability to accomplish my vision."

As her coach, I believed fully in Chloe's abilities. She was bright, conservative in her financial habits, thorough, and passionate—and I can't say enough about that last ingredient. Passion is significant fuel that helps you persevere despite obstacles, fear, and discouragement. If you are passionate about a goal, you can tap into that passion as a source of energy that will see you through to the finish line.

At the core of Chloe's lack of confidence was her persistent doubt about her ability and know-how to see each goal through to completion. Whether her doubt was well-founded or not didn't matter because she believed it was true.

And "you are what you think" is not just a cute little saying. It's a Bible-based truth: "For as he thinks in his heart, so is he" (Proverbs 23:7, NKJV).

Your thoughts can give you confidence or sap it.

Chloe's dilemma brings to light a key building block of confidence—trusting yourself to be able to do the thing you want to do. You need the resolve to do what you have to do to accomplish the goals you've set before yourself. There's no time to wonder *if* you can accomplish the purposes of God for your life. You must make up your mind to do it! You must commit yourself to persevering and learning whatever you need to learn.

It can be a very good thing to surround yourself, the way Chloe did, with people who know more than you do about a particular topic. Just remember not to give your power to them as though what you know and what you sense from God in your spirit is not as important as their input. You don't have to know everything to succeed. You just have to know where to find answers—and with tenacity, patience, and perseverance, you will find them.

This type of attitude rejects fear as an excuse for not being confident—and it belongs to a person who admits her own shortcomings and is comfortable enough with those shortcomings to seek guidance when needed, yet to trust herself to ultimately be able to acquire the knowledge, skills, or whatever she might need for a particular situation.

In essence, trusting one's own potential is an opportunity to build character—the type of character that says, "No matter the circumstances, I have the ability, with God, to make wise decisions and to see my goals through to completion."

Confidence Prayer

God, I want to be a person of my word. Philippians 4:13 promises that "I can do everything through him who gives me strength." Strengthen my resolve to complete what I start—and continue to strengthen my decision-making skills so that I start things I am passionate about doing.

Confidence Journal

What don't you trust yourself to do right now? What step will you take toward trusting yourself to do exactly that?

Confidence Builder

Today, identify something small that you have previously not trusted yourself to see through to the end. Perhaps you need to determine to lose weight, to start investing, or to do something entirely different. Set a small goal regarding the issue. (For example, rather than setting a goal of losing fifty pounds, you start with a goal of five pounds and then adjust the goal after you achieve the first one.) The point of this exercise is to build up your stick-to-it muscle so that you can trust yourself to see something through to completion.

Day 20

Be Willing to Fail

> Enduring my failures and then learning from them has given me confidence to try things I never would've tried if I was set on being perfect.
>
> —Ronnie, 34

Have you ever had one of those embarrassing public moments when you wished you could press a rewind button and try again?

On a ski trip to Vail, Colorado, in the early nineties, my friend Christie and I took some brush-up ski lessons and headed for the lift that would take us to the bunny slopes. Although we both lived in Colorado at the time, we were novice skiers and a little nervous about trying to get off the ski lift without looking like novices. As I watched a couple of children in front of us effortlessly glide out of their seats and down the short incline, I thought, *This will be a piece of cake.*

Our seat approached the spot where we were to get off, and I cautiously waited for some sort of signal or a little push from the seat that would tell me it was time to stand up and ski off. Christie, recognizing that no such signal or push exists, stood up, lost her balance as well as her ski poles, and was smacked in the rear end by the moving seat as I looked on in astonishment.

It was like a comedy scene in slow motion as it suddenly occurred to me, *Val, there is no signal. You were supposed to just get up!*

But now it was too late. I had missed my three-second window of opportunity to get off the lift, and now I was stuck gliding along as the seat made a U-turn to head back down the mountain. At this point, I was too high above the ground to jump. Christie was sprawled out in the snow paralyzed by a fit of laughter, and the passengers behind us were yelling for the operator to stop the lift.

With all the commotion, skiers along the mountainside stopped in their tracks and were pointing at me from what seemed like every direction. Even my father, a hundred yards away on much steeper slopes, stopped to check out the scene, only to see his daughter being coaxed down by the ski-lift operator who caught me as I made my leap off the seat.

Years later I still laugh every time I think about it. What a valuable lesson about how important it is to seize your window of opportunity!

Is there an opportunity in your life right now that you need to take the initiative to pursue, but you are hesitant and waiting on some sort of signal to push you toward it because you lack the confidence to just go for it?

While it's nice to get a push every once in a while, I've found that you'll miss your window of opportunity if you don't act at the right time to close the gap between where you are now and where you want to be. It's scary to try new things, but fear shouldn't keep you from going for it.

Christie may have looked less than graceful getting off the ski lift, but she still made it off. She didn't hesitate. She went for it, and—fall or no fall—she made it.

I, on the other hand, was thinking too hard, analyzing the situation, and waiting for some elusive perfect moment. I was afraid of getting hurt, doing it wrong, or looking ridiculous. In the end, I did it wrong and looked ridiculous anyway!

The same thing happens when we venture into new territory in life. So sometimes you have to let go of your fear of doing it wrong, looking ridiculous, or getting hurt. You have to stop analyzing and just go for it. Think of it as a leap of faith—an opportunity to conquer your fear, take back your power. When a window of opportunity opens in certain areas of your life, it is essential that you seize the moment.

What window of opportunity do you need to take advantage of right now?

A reader e-mailed me to ask this question recently. She told me, "I've always known that my husband has been called to pastor. I believe in him and know he's well equipped to do it. We also have always known that I would co-pastor. Well, now he believes that it's time for us to step out and do it, and I have fear. I don't want to fail. This is such an enormous task, and people's lives are at stake. What should I do? I don't want to mess up, but I don't want to miss God either. Help!"

The answer is simple, although the path may be uncomfortable. I had to tell her, "Step out in faith! If God called you to do it, you cannot fail. It's not possible! You may not do it perfectly, but anything you fail at, God will use as a learning tool to teach you to get better and to build character. Fear is just a part of the process. This will all be a part of your testimony. The mistake that keeps many people stuck is believing that because they feel fear, they should not move forward."

When you're moving to the next level or into a new arena in life, you'll feel fear. It's natural. God doesn't say we won't feel fear. Instead, throughout the Bible, He tells us repeatedly that we are to have courage. First

Chronicles 28:20 says, "Be strong and of good courage, and do it; do not fear nor be dismayed, for the LORD God—my God—will be with you" (NKJV). He is with you. Courage isn't the absence of fear—it's the ability to move forward despite the presence of fear!

Remember, this calling isn't about you. It's about what God wants to do through you. Don't get in the way by allowing fear (the enemy) to keep you from your destiny!

When it comes to windows of opportunity, sometimes you are blessed with a second chance. When I was stuck in my seat, having missed my opportunity to get off the ski lift, I got a second chance when the operator stopped the lift and helped me down. I think of it as a metaphor for how God gives us the grace to make mistakes and still reach our goals. Despite the rough start, Christie and I had so much fun skiing that day—and we enjoyed the chance to laugh at ourselves. If your window of opportunity opens for a second time, take advantage of it.

Some of the reasons you may hesitate include these fears:

- You won't do it right.
- You'll look bad.
- You won't do it perfectly.
- You'll fall.
- You'll get hurt.
- You'll lose control.
- You don't know enough yet.

Notice two things in particular about all these reasons for hesitating. First, fear is always at the root of hesitation and paralysis. Your confidence will always suffer when you forget that the Lord is with you wherever you go. Second, though, notice the word that opens each line: *you.* All of these reasons are about you and how you are going to look or be impacted. Many people miss out on the blessings God has for them because they are too self-centered to take the focus off what they can do and instead begin focusing on what God can do—in them, through them, and for them.

"Pride goes before destruction, a haughty spirit before a fall," Proverbs 16:18 promises. Often those who appear most confident by worldly standards are the most prideful. They will only do those things that make them look good and that benefit them. If a particular activity could leave them vulnerable, they avoid it even if they feel divinely inspired to do it. "But you don't understand," they'll say. "I don't know how to do that."

Confidence Prayer

When You say, "Go," Lord, I want to step out in faith without hesitation! I need confidence to do that. Second Timothy 1:7 tells me You have not given me "a spirit of timidity, but a spirit of power, of love and of self-discipline." Today, I commit myself to taking a leap of faith that You've been nudging me to take. It feels scary. I might fall. I might do it wrong. People may point and laugh. But that's okay, Lord! If I am following Your path for me, I know I cannot fail.

Confidence Journal

What are you waiting on? Explore this in your journal today: what is God calling you to step out in faith and do today?

Confidence Builder

It's time. You've been waiting long enough. This is your second chance. Today is the day to make an important decision. Take that leap of faith.

Day 21

Know the Real You

> Everything today is about the cover-up or makeover. Everything is so superficial that people don't know what the truth is about anything—not even about themselves. No one seems to really want to deal with the reality of life. Even reality TV is a joke.
>
> —Ashley, 28

Our culture often is not based on authenticity. It's based on what you present to the world—and we're told daily how we should look, behave, spend our money, and live.

One afternoon in 2000, I was sitting in my office when a friend called me, enthusiastic about a concert he'd been to at a local spot the night before. The singer was Macy Gray, whom I'd not heard of before, and I wondered why he felt compelled to call me specifically to talk about this concert. My friend, who is British and not black, said he loved her hair and was wondering if I'd ever considered wearing my hair like hers.

"Her hair is really great," he said. "Can your hair do that?"

"Do what?" I asked, trying to imagine what "that" was.

"Well, it's not exactly an afro, but it's big and curly and really cool," he explained and suggested I go onto her Web site to see a picture while we were talking. "I mean, does she have special hair, or did she do something special to keep it from being straight like yours?"

I chuckled. He was really curious about it, and for obvious reasons he had no clue about black people's hair, so I proceeded to explain.

"I have a relaxer," I told him.

"A relaxer?" he said amused by the word that suggests my hair is tense and needs some relaxation.

"Yes," I said. "It makes my hair straight."

"So your hair could do what Macy Gray's does, but you straighten it out?" he probed.

"Yes, I suppose it could," I said looking at her picture on the computer screen and trying to imagine the reaction I might get if I showed up at a client meeting with that hairdo. "My mom gave me an afro once and had pictures taken when I was three years old so she could have a keepsake, I guess, from the seventies," I joked. "Other than that, my hair's never come close to this look."

"So is a relaxer a one-time thing, or is it like hair color where you have to keep getting it done?" he asked, sincerely interested in understanding the process, but apparently perplexed by it.

"Well, everyone's hair is different, but generally a woman who has a relaxer will get one about every six to eight weeks," I said.

"So is that what all black women do?" he asked, overwhelmed by the idea that millions of women he sees every day have altered the state of their hair.

"No, not all," I said. "There are a lot of different hair types, but I would venture to say that a very large percentage of African American females straighten their hair—most with relaxers, but some use other means."

"Well, why do you do that? Why don't you just wear it the way it grows out of your head?" he asked with childlike wonder.

I was stumped. This simple question shifted my perspective. Some choices and habits that you make are so ingrained that you never think about why you do them. You just do! It's what you've always done. In many cases, our habits and behaviors are rooted in a fear of being rejected by others. We're taught that who we are may not be acceptable, so we must create a persona that is acceptable.

People who took the confidence survey spoke of feeling that everyone is walking around wearing a mask. I would venture to say that even when you don't recognize that you are wearing a mask, you very well may be.

It's not until you see yourself from a different perspective that you recognize the behaviors that constitute your mask.

My conversation with my friend is a simple illustration of how easy and quick it can be to alter your state of being without really knowing why you do what you do. I'm not suggesting that you should stop going to the salon—for a relaxer or color or a cut or whatever. I am suggesting, however, that you should question the things you do so that you can better understand your purpose behind the choices you make. Authentic people understand their values and align their actions with them.

When my friend asked me, "Why don't you just wear your hair the way it grows out of your head?" I was stumped. I thought about it for a long time.

There was the obvious answer: My hair is easier to deal with when it's relaxed. Also, I'd had a relaxer since I was six years old, so I really didn't know what my natural hair was like.

I pondered his question long after the conversation ended. *Why do I relax my hair?* I wanted to know. The possible answers were bothersome. *Is it because the standard of beauty in our culture is based on European traits, not African ones—or anything non-European, for that matter?*

Long, straight, blond hair is lifted up as the culture's standard of beauty—preferable on a curvy, size 6, five-foot-eight body. It's not just African American women who struggle to measure up to the standard. But the curly, shorter hair that tends to grow from my head is rarely celebrated.

Have I bought into cultural brainwashing about my hair? Is this why I've worn weaves and hairpieces off and on since high school? Is this the reason I've always hated to see the new growth sprouting forth weeks after a relaxer, revealing my true roots and sending me rushing to the salon for a touch-up to straighten out those kinks?

These self-curiosity questions challenged me. I was honest with myself that I'd had a hate-hate relationship with my hair since I was about twelve. That was the year a bad relaxer caused my soft, shoulder-length hair to break off. As you probably remember, puberty's not the best time to start having issues with your looks, so it was traumatic for me.

What I learned from my conversation with my friend that day several years ago took me on an inward journey. I considered cutting my hair all off and going natural, but I didn't feel led to that course of action. But I began making a conscious choice to love and appreciate my hair just as it was because it is a blessing from God to have any at all. I'd had a conversation with friend and fellow author Priscilla Shirer, who—after years of frustration straightening her hair with chemicals—decided to start over from scratch.

Fearful but determined, Priscilla cut her hair down to an inch or two of unrelaxed hair and let it grow out. To her delightful surprise, the texture of her natural hair is beautiful and curly, and it's now longer and healthier than it ever was before.

"I just had to learn how to work with my own hair," she told me on the phone one day.

After much soul-searching, I decided that the issue was not about insecurity or buying into cultural pressures as much as it was about it being an easier choice for me on a day-to-day basis. But I made a significant shift from *There's something wrong with my hair* to *It's just easier to have it styled the way I do, and I like it.*

It was a choice—an *authentic* choice for me.

The lesson in this story is that we often don't even recognize that we're wearing a mask. How can I be real when I don't really know who I am? And sometimes we don't see our own mask because it is so automatic, so ingrained.

Why not fully express yourself in every aspect of your life—at your work, at home, in relationships, and even through your material possessions such as your choice of clothing and car? Be yourself, and present your authentic self to the world. When you are unapologetically your authentic self, you are most confident. It takes time to be intentionally authentic in your choices. Many people just do what everyone else is doing and buy what the commercials tell them to buy. Start noticing how you may be inclined to accept uncritically "the ways things have always been done."

Question things. And when others question you, try not to immediately become defensive. You never know when God is challenging your thought process through the words of others.

This book is about you making some shifts in your life. It's about shifting to a place of certainty that whatever you do, as long as you are courageous enough to surrender to God's will, you will succeed.

Actually, it takes less courage to follow God's path because "nothing is impossible with God" (Luke 1:37). I have no confidence in my strength alone. I have unstoppable confidence in God's strength.

As each day you build authentic confidence in your relationships, work, finances, health, and spiritual life, your awareness of yourself and understanding of your choices will heighten. You'll notice the ways in which you engage in habits and behaviors that are fear-based and not authentically you. As you grasp this new knowledge of yourself, dig deep to understand your motivations. Seek the truth about what you really want from yourself—and why.

Confidence Prayer

Lord, help me see more of myself. Make me aware of the ways in which my behaviors are not aligned with the authenticity of who You created me to be. Give me the courage to answer the questions about why I do what I do that cause me to feel like running in the other direction. Help me find the way of life that will work best for me.

Confidence Journal

What behaviors or habits do you exhibit that could be interpreted as either not authentically you or masking the true you? Explain why you engage in these habits or behaviors. What kinds of changes in these habits or behaviors, if any, do you need to make?

Confidence Builder

Identify one way in which you can embrace an aspect of yourself that you have previously rejected. Embrace it today. For example, you could choose an aspect of your looks such as your hair, size, or skin, or you could choose something unrelated to your looks. I embraced my hair by running my fingers through it, acknowledging its unique beauty, and saying a prayer of thanks that God had blessed me with it.

Day 22

Get Off the Self-Esteem Roller Coaster

> I may not be all that I want to be, but I know the Master Potter is continuing to mold and shape me into a perfect vessel to be used for His glory.
>
> —Belinda, 55

You're a spiritual being having a human experience. When you begin to believe that who you are is based on what you do, what you look like, or what your various roles are in life, your confidence and worth will be in question when those aspects of your life change.

Today I'd like to share a conversation with three women—readers like you—who struggled with doubts about their worth and who asked specific questions about how to overcome those doubts. I invite you to glean the following lessons.

Scenario 1: If you don't value yourself, you'll attract people who follow your lead.

Scenario 2: The tragedies of life threaten to completely knock us down, but if you survive, there is a reason. God has a plan and purpose for your life—and your greatest purpose may be born from your greatest pain.

Scenario 3: A chip on your shoulder results in a chip in your confidence. Your perception is not always reality. You can sabotage your own success not only by doubting yourself, but by doubting and judging others without just cause.

Scenario 1: The Self-Esteem Roller Coaster

A twenty-two-year-old woman once told me she really needed some guidelines for how to live her life to the fullest. "I know I have a major problem with self-esteem," she admitted. "Sometimes it's high, other times it's low; and when it comes to my love life, I usually gravitate to the wrong kind of men and end up disappointed because I'm not treated well. The cycle happens over and over again."

If you've ever found yourself riding such a roller coaster, then you'll know this to be true: if you allow others to define your value, you'll always be on a wild ride. When others are happy with you, your self-esteem is high. When they don't like you or something about you, you feel bad about yourself.

But you're valuable simply because you are here.

So make a decision to love yourself unconditionally. Spend time alone, meditate on God's Word, and pamper yourself. Give yourself permission to go after what you want—and pursue it with passion. Your possibilities are unlimited.

You'll find that you teach others how to treat you by how you treat yourself—so to live your life to the fullest, learn to live in the moment and to live with purpose. Don't haphazardly enter relationships. (I call getting involved in relationships, jobs, and situations just because they cross your path living by accident.) Be willing to pass up the wrong people so you can make room for the right ones.

Scenario 2: Hitting Rock Bottom

A thirty-seven-year-old single woman tells of her son who was killed two years ago at the age of fifteen. Since his death, she's felt her life is useless. "I don't have any faith in anything," she says. "I don't know what keeps me going because nothing in my life works out right for me no matter what I do. I want to be happy, but how? I stopped dating altogether because I'm afraid to be close to anyone. I have no confidence that anything will ever go right again, but I'm willing to try. Does God still have a plan for my life?"

Of course! God indeed has a plan, but there's no doubt that losing a son to death has meant intense pain over the last two years. When you've experienced such a loss, it's bound to affect your confidence—and it's important to give yourself a grieving period.

It's equally important to make the decision to begin moving forward again. At some point. Moving forward doesn't mean forgetting your child or telling yourself you have to "get over it." You can never do that. But life does not become useless even after such a profound loss.

If you're alive, God has a purpose for your life. Make the choice to seek and fulfill that purpose. It can be very natural for mothers to believe that their purpose is simply being a mother, but our purpose is not our family role, a job, or certain achievements. Instead, our purpose is about how we make a difference in others' lives in the process of embodying those roles.

God blessed this mother with life, and her son's death illustrates just how precious life is. For you, there may have been another kind of pain and loss underscoring the value of another kind of blessing. Why not honor that blessing by making the most of the precious life you've been given? Maybe you could discover newfound joy and purpose by encouraging people who have lost something similar or by inspiring others to make the most of the life they have.

We each can find purpose even in our most painful experiences by exploring some helpful, key questions:

- What's the most meaningful way that I can preserve the legacy of this loss in my life?
- What are the ten blessings I'm most grateful for?
- If I could paint a picture of a more joyful life three months from now, what would I have to do differently to bring that vision to life?

Now notice how your words can uplift you or bring you down. When this grieving mother said things such as, "My life is useless" and "Nothing works out right for me no matter what I do," she steals hope from her own spirit and speaks a self-fulfilling prophecy. Even if you feel that way, practice saying the opposite. Keep the memory of your blessing alive, but don't allow its legacy to be one of hopelessness and despair. Make the decision to work with the Lord to strengthen your faith through this trial rather than allowing it to be diminished.

Scenario 3: Perception Reality Check

One of my clients, a thirty-one-year-old woman, told me she was employed by a well-known pharmacy in my city, where she'd worked since she was fifteen years old. She'd recently received a big promotion. Great, right?

No, she said. She feared she'd be treated unfairly in her new position because she felt she had three strikes against her going in the door: she was female, the only black person in the company, and the youngest employee in the department.

Even though this woman knew she was good at her job, she couldn't help feeling insecure because she felt like a token. "Help me put these feelings to rest so I can show them what a young, intelligent black woman can do," she pleaded.

Have you ever been in a similar situation? In today's world, assumptions of prejudice in the workplace can do more to hurt your career than help it.

Give your employers the benefit of the doubt. And realize that if you assume your race, gender, and age are strikes against you, then you'll look for reasons to believe you're being unfairly treated. Prejudice of all sorts can be an unfortunate reality, but anticipating it without just cause can alienate you from your employer and, as a result, limit your advancement. So don't carry your race, age, and gender like baggage that weighs you down.

Be excellent at what you do, and deliver results that speak for themselves. Those who excel don't waste time focusing on what negative things might happen. You can instead take confidence in who you are and what you've done.

Confidence Prayer

Lord, in the ups and downs of life, give me stability of mind and emotions. Help me perceive truth in difficult circumstances where my perception may be skewed. Despite the trials I face, let me not lose confidence in You and Your purpose for my life. Help me always remember that I am not what happens to me.

I am a spiritual being having a human experience—and at times the human experience will pain my spirit. In those moments, I want to take refuge in Your arms, Lord. Thank You for Your promise to always be with me, wherever I go.

Confidence Journal

In what ways do you devalue who you are, and what can you do to change that tendency?

Confidence Builder

Today, do something to celebrate you—something that makes you feel especially good and significant and valuable. Enjoy!

Day 23

Develop Cross-Confidence

> I can successfully manage a sizeable budget at work and make lots of money for my employer, yet I hesitate to make important decisions about money on a personal level. I'm afraid I'll lose it all.
>
> —Diane, 36

Have you ever noticed that while your confidence about one aspect of your life may wane, it soars in another? If you haven't noticed, I want you to begin noticing. Tapping into the power—and sometimes the momentum—of having confidence in one area of your life can help you access confidence in another area. I call it cross-confidence.

During my first coaching session with Kecia, she confided her deep desire for her family to own their own home and her desire to earn more money. A college administrator with a master's degree, she had the background to achieve her goals, but—in her words—she had been "playing small" her whole life.

"When do you want to buy a home?" I asked.

"Oh, I just don't know if we can afford it," she replied. "And I hate to admit it, but I feel like that's something other people can have, but not me. I know that's not true, but it's how I feel."

"Who told you that?" I asked, curious where she might have picked up this limiting belief.

She told me that she feared what family members (specifically her mom) might think if she "played a bigger game" and began to manifest signs of outward success. Afraid those close to her might suddenly feel distanced from her if she succeeded at higher levels, Kecia had smothered her dreams in order to prevent the potential conflict or disapproval. She made a decision, though, to begin creating the life she wanted for herself rather than the life she perceived others wanting her to live. She set the goal of saving enough to buy a new home within two years.

Throughout the first year, Kecia began to transform her thinking and build her confidence based on what she really wanted. In the process, she began to see herself differently. Within three months, she'd started investing her money intentionally and increased her savings by hundreds of dollars each month in preparation for a down payment. During the time that she became more intentional with her money, Hurricane Katrina hit her state. Although she lived nearly a hundred miles from the coast, the hurricane's devastating impact on her city had a profound impact on her personally. She realized that her yearning to be intentional in her life was also about having the resources to handle with confidence whatever life threw her way. Within six months, she landed a new, higher-paying job in a neighboring state where most of her relatives lived. She and her husband were able to relocate, and Kecia soon realized that a home purchase was within reach.

Within nine months of first acknowledging she wanted to buy a house, she and her husband closed on their own home.

As Kecia transformed her thinking about what was possible in each area of her life, she gained the confidence to move forward in new areas. Intentional investing and saving sparked the confidence to do something about the size of her paycheck. Increasing her income by getting a new job boosted her confidence in her ability to achieve the dream of home ownership.

Seeing her own transformation in these areas led her to ask, *Where else is my life out of alignment with who I am and what I really want?*

After nine months of forward movement and success, Kecia was confident about her ability to change her circumstances through her choices. As she pondered her life, she realized it was time to release the weight she'd gained over the years.

"It didn't happen all at once," she said. "Maybe ten pounds a year. It was gradual enough that I didn't notice how significant the change was."

Attempts in the past to lose weight had been based on external pressures such as fitting into a size 10 dress or losing weight for a reunion. But those reasons weren't inspiring enough to sustain a long-term lifestyle change.

This time around, though, Kecia was interested in making a change: "Because I deserve to be healthy."

She focused on appreciating and caring for the temple of the Holy Spirit with which she had been blessed and took full responsibility for her eating and exercise choices.

Today, she shops intentionally, exercises five days each week, has cut her sugary snack intake by 75 percent, and plans meals for the entire week rather than opting for fast-food purchases on the way home from work.

She's well on her way to her goal.

When we first began coaching, Kecia wanted to make healthy lifestyle changes, but she wasn't ready. As she made changes in other areas of her life, her confidence that she could indeed make a permanent lifestyle change in the area of her health and her weight grew.

As you notice the areas of your life in which you lack confidence, have patience. Cross-confidence can be your strongest asset. It's rare that only one area of our lives can use some improvement. So start in an area in which you can make progress that will bolster your confidence and strengthen your faith in God and in the strength and guidance He offers.

As your confidence grows, identify the character traits you had to call on in order to experience growth or success—and notice how God helped you. Realize the power you have to make decisions that can transform your everyday life. Then allow what you have observed about yourself to give you the confidence to tackle another area of your life.

Cross-confidence is letting the strengths you displayed in one area of life bolster your confidence to grow in an area where you are less sure of yourself. Small steps in the direction of your vision build momentum. As you succeed, you'll increase your confidence in your ability to push forward even further—sometimes in new areas.

In what area of your life do you have the most confidence? Take some time to answer the following questions. These six questions are a self-coaching exercise.

Identify something you accomplished which required authentic confidence.

____

____

What about you or the circumstances empowered you to achieve this accomplishment? List every factor you can think of.

____

____

____

Now take a moment to identify something important to you for which you lack confidence.

____

____

What would give you confidence in this situation where you lack it? List every confidence builder you can think of.

____

____

____

What would you need to do to take advantage of the confidence builders you listed above?

____

____

____

What character traits enabled you to accomplish the thing you mentioned in response to question 1? In what ways can these traits give you confidence in the area you identified in response to question 4?

____

____

____

I want you to start noticing what gives you confidence and then find ways to be similarly confident in the areas of your life where you lack it. Consider the things you have accomplished that others lack the confidence to do. Don't disregard your confidence in any area. Recognize that your confidence might just transform your life if you dig deeply enough to transfer that confidence to another area of your life.

As Kecia experienced when she finally decided to develop a healthy and fit lifestyle, momentum from having confidence in one area can cross over into another. Until she saw the results that came from the new choices she'd begun making in her work, family, and financial life, she lacked the confidence that she had the power to do anything different in the area of health and fitness.

Building long-term, authentic confidence is a process. As you discover the reserves of your own strength, you will stand more completely in who you are.

For example, I used to be a horrible procrastinator—and it seemed to manifest itself most obviously in my writing. And it didn't begin just when I started writing books. Ever since I remember writing—probably back to my first research paper in middle school—I always procrastinated. I'd begin with the intention of getting started early, but somehow I wouldn't get started until it was much too late. Then, feeling the pressure of possibly failing to meet my deadline, I would sprint to the finish.

Clearly, the adrenaline rush was the tool I used to get things done. I wanted to change, but I didn't have the confidence to believe I actually could.

Have you ever declared you would make a change, but deep down a persistent doubt let you know that you probably didn't have what it took to do so? That doubt isn't something that's nice to admit, but sometimes it's the reality. I'd failed so many times before when I had set out to start early and make consistent, joyful progress all the way to the finish line. Why would this time be any different? My doubts proved true.

It wasn't until I managed to master change in two other areas of my life—consistently working out and building a stronger financial foundation—that I gained the confidence to master change in the area of procrastination. The changes I'd made in those other areas took discipline, perseverance, and intentional planning—the very character traits needed to overcome my procrastination habit.

Confidence Prayer

Lord, open my eyes to the ways I have already succeeded. Help me see the character traits I have developed in the process of persevering through challenges and living purposefully. Then, God, help me apply the lessons I've learned and the confidence I've developed to those areas of my life in which I lack confidence. I can see now that I am closer to some of my goals than I previously realized because You have been molding, shaping, and developing me to accomplish Your purposes for my life.

Confidence Journal

Review the list of character traits you listed in response to question 6 above. Which one is most meaningful to you? How could this particular trait help you achieve an unmet goal in an area where you lack confidence? Be specific.

Confidence Builder

Today, identify something you've been wanting to do, but have hesitated to do because of fear. Do it today—or if it is impossible to do it today, schedule a time, and ask a friend or family member to hold you accountable for doing it.

Day 24

Take the Initiative

> I finally figured out that if I didn't like the way my life was going, I needed to stop complaining and do something about it. It's that simple. I went back to school to study something I am passionate about and transitioned into a new career. I make more money now. It wasn't easy and it didn't happen overnight, but it was worth it. And boy, did it give me a confidence boost.
>
> —JEN, 34

It was another frustrating day at work for Carla. A public relations manager for a highly successful big-city law firm, she often felt the work she was doing served no purpose other than making wealthy people wealthier. And the bosses she supported seemed almost soulless to her. Everything was about money.

By the time she called for her coaching session on this day, she'd had it.

"There's no integrity here," she complained. "People feel they can talk to me any kind of way they want to, and I'm tired of being treated like this." Carla sounded depleted and small.

Despite her salary being four times that of the national median family income, her position left her feeling less than valued. These words she spoke to me reinforced what I could already hear in her voice.

Office politics were threatening Carla's job and leaving her unsure of what would be next for her. But she was afraid to go to the powers that be and speak up for herself. We used the coaching session to devise a plan of action. She needed to be direct, yet respectful. And she needed to know where she stood with the company. Although her job performance was excellent, it appeared someone wanted to bring in a new woman to replace her and have her work in a subservient role to the new person.

Carla had spent the previous week observing the new woman coming in for an interview and meeting her colleagues. The management—which should have been responsible for cluing her in about their plans—pretended everything was normal.

"It's humiliating to have a co-worker come to your office and ask you if you are being displaced," she sighed. "It's even worse when you can't answer their question because your bosses have left you in the dark."

"What do you want right now?" I asked during our coaching session.

"I want them to be up-front enough to tell me what's going on," she said. "Do I need to start looking for another job?"

"What else do you want to know?" I continued, listening for the essence of what she really wanted from her employer.

"You know what? I just want respect," she said. "I want to work in a place where people appreciate all of my hard work and the talent I bring to my position. And what I really want is to make a difference, and I realize that no matter how hard I work for these people, whether they appreciate me or not, the mission of this firm is not about making the world a better place."

"So I hear you saying that you really don't want to work here anyway. Is that accurate?" I asked.

She paused for a long moment.

"Yeah. That's right. The situation I find myself in with my employer right now is consistent with how they operate. I've seen them do it to other people. Their values just don't line up with mine. They cross all sorts of boundaries with me—and I let them do it, which makes me mad at myself for not standing up for myself."

"Is it possible, then, that what you're dealing with is something much bigger than someone being hired over you in your department?" I asked.

After pondering for a moment, she responded, "Absolutely. This is about me standing up for myself, setting healthier boundaries, asking for what I want, and going after what I want."

Over the course of our coaching sessions, Carla realized that people treated her the way she allowed them to treat her. The light bulb came on. It wasn't just about her relationships at work. This same pattern could be seen in her personal relationships as well. Carla decided to take a step toward standing up for herself by scheduling a meeting with her boss. She prepared in advance by determining what she most wanted from the conversation:

- to know their intentions for her
- to express her concern over how the transition was being handled
- to request a new position that she found more desirable

"It feels so empowering to stop being the victim and to take the initiative to start the conversation that everyone has been tiptoeing around," she said energetically after taking that first step of scheduling a meeting with her boss.

Because Carla now understood her truth—that she really didn't want to work at the company anyway—she was also less worried about the possibility that things would not work out long-term. She realized that her desire was to take steps that would empower her to leave the firm within one year and free her to pursue work that was more purposeful and more aligned with her values. Acknowledging her true desire gave her confidence as she realized that she had the power to make changes that would create a more fulfilling life.

Here's what Carla did, and you can use this same process to take the initiative on any issue that leaves you feeling powerless and unequipped to change your circumstances:

- *Dig deep to discover the message God has for you in the situation.*
- *Get to the essence of the God-given opportunity to stretch yourself and become a more powerful you.* It may be time for you to stand up for yourself in a bigger way.
- *Take the initiative to have a conversation that needs to take place.* Be ready to make requests that need to be made in order for you to feel better about yourself.
- *Look toward the future.* The lessons learned from the situation are likely steppingstones toward a more confident way of being. Identify the other ways you need to apply the lessons you learned to other areas of your life.

It's amazing how easily you can find yourself in a rut and bogged down by the belief that you don't have a choice about your circumstances. When you embrace authentic confidence, though, you let go of your victim status—of the belief that your life happens at the whim of others. You let go of excuses and find solutions.

Excuses diminish your confidence. Excuses imply that you are powerless over your own circumstances, and that all things are not working together for your good. Anytime we feel powerless, we lack confidence.

Have you ever found yourself having to fix a problem someone else created? That kind of situation can be extremely frustrating. Often it leads to a cycle of blaming and complaining. Well, I feel led to share a few words of inspiration for those areas of life in which you feel like a victim of your circumstances. There is an element of confidence that comes from the conviction that you have the ability to change the course of your life. It's the concept I mentioned earlier: self-efficacy.

You can be absolutely right in a given situation. Perhaps someone else *is* to blame, but blaming doesn't get you any closer to fixing a problem or overcoming a challenge. I have found that you can get to the other side of your challenge a lot faster if you change your focus: Let go of blame and grudges. Then forge ahead to do whatever you must do to resolve it.

We cannot control everything that happens to us, but we can control how we respond to it. One of the most important aspects of spiritual growth is choosing to focus on a solution rather than on who is to blame.

When you blame others, you are essentially saying, "Other people determine my destiny. Others determine my happiness, my goals, and my future." Whatever happens in your life, taking responsibility for it empowers you to learn and to do better in the future.

Sometimes, as hard as it is to admit, other people are not the only ones to blame. It is freeing to admit our own culpability in the problems we face. It's okay to be wrong or make a mistake sometimes. As humans, it's part of who we are—imperfect beings. Mistakes are often the best way for us to learn, though. So instead of trying to cover up or pretend that a mistake either didn't happen or wasn't your fault, why not ask, "What could I do differently next time?"

When I wanted to write a book years ago but never got around to it, I always blamed my business and a lack of time. But you know what? Blaming my schedule was useless. It didn't get the book written. Instead, it justified my not writing it. It wasn't until I got tired of blaming my schedule that I finally put pen to paper and wrote.

So be honest with yourself. Are you blaming someone or something for circumstances you don't like in your life? Do you find yourself blaming your employer for financial challenges because you aren't paid enough? Do you blame your family for problems? Do you blame the world for not opening doors of opportunity for you? Whether or not someone else is to blame for our circumstances, we don't move any closer to our goals by blaming and complaining. In fact, life is often waiting on us to simply accept responsibility, learn the lessons God has for us, and exercise our faith that He can help us change the circumstances. Perhaps that's the lesson He is offering you today: It doesn't really matter how you got to this point—whether in your finances, a relationship, your health, or your work. What really matters is that you learn what you are meant to learn and that you persevere to the next level on your journey.

Confidence Prayer

Sometimes life simply does not seem fair, God. But help me always accept responsibility and take the initiative to resolve challenges as they arise. Give me the energy and the integrity to do this in a way that is pleasing to You. Help me let go of selfish pride that blinds me from the truth of a situation. Grant me the courage to step in a new direction when You allow a door to close. Proverbs 3:5–6 tells me to trust in You with all my heart and lean not on my own understanding. It tells me that in all my ways I am to acknowledge You and that You shall direct my paths. Thank You for guiding me, loving me, and building my trust in You day by day.

Confidence Journal

In what area of your life do you most need to accept responsibility and shift your focus to resolving an issue? Be specific. What can you do differently in that situation?

Confidence Builder

Today, refuse to play the blame game. When you feel tempted to blame someone else, stop yourself and ask yourself these questions: What responsibility do I have in this situation? What action would empower me to take control of the situation rather than being left feeling like a victim of circumstances?

Day 25

Make Wise Decisions

What gives me confidence is knowing that I've made the right decision.

—PHYLLIS, 40

In the summer of 1993, just as I was about to graduate from Florida State University, I made a decision that turned out to a very wise one. Until about a year before I finished college, I was sure I wanted to be an international corporate attorney. I made that decision in the tenth grade based on fairly limited information. My major was international affairs, I grew up learning German and Spanish, and law seemed a logical choice. But as mentioned earlier, when I began to learn more about my planned career path, it just didn't appeal to me as the best fit for my interests.

So I decided to apply to a new graduate program in journalism at Florida A&M University, just a mile away from FSU. I was unsure of exactly what I wanted to do with a master's degree in journalism, but I was excited by the possibilities. But the month before I was to begin the program, I began to doubt.

Maybe an MBA would be better, I thought. *I'll move back home to Denver and pursue that.*

I was twenty years old, this was a major life decision, and I wasn't confident about how to make it. But I packed up and prepared to move. Just as I was ready to go, a letter arrived from Florida A&M University's journalism school, and it offered a full-tuition scholarship and a graduate assistantship.

I stood in the living room of my one-bedroom apartment filled with boxes packed and ready to ship to Colorado. *What should I do?* I wondered. Something in my spirit said, *Unpack and stay. It's not time to leave Tallahassee yet.*

I listened to that—and as I look back on my decision, I realize divine intervention steered me onto my unique path. The truth is, I had no idea just how that particular course of study would impact my career. From my work as a marketing director, to running my own public relations firm, to writing books and columns, to serving as a host in radio and television, only God clearly knew what kind of training would be best for the professional vision He had in store for me. I'm just thankful that I listened to Him.

Sometimes the decisions we make seem obvious, but at other times our decisions can be difficult and confusing. So how can you cut through the confusion and open your ears to hear divine intervention when God speaks?

These twelve questions can help you make wise, confident decisions—whether big or small—in your career, relationships, finances, and health. Too often we can get into the habit of making emotional or hasty decisions. When we do so, we don't feel confident about those decisions because they've not been made on a solid foundation of thoughtfulness and wisdom.

James 1:5 tells us, "If any of you lacks wisdom, he should ask God, who gives generously to all without finding fault, and it will be given to him."

If you can manage your decisions well, you will prosper professionally, personally, financially, and emotionally. Consider a decision you have been pondering or perhaps even feeling unsure about making and then ask yourself these questions:

1. *Is now the time to make this decision?* Timing is key when it comes to good decisions. You must be willing to move when it's time to move and to be patient when it's time to be still. Have the courage to wait for God's timing. Don't force a decision. Allow it to come naturally. Clearly, some decisions must be made quickly, but don't be hasty. You can still gather facts, consider your alternatives, pray, and make a wise decision.
2. *What's the purpose anyway?* Why you would be doing something is the fuel that drives your decision. Make sure you are making decisions out of pure motives. Also be clear about why the decision needs to be made and what objective will be met by making it.
3. *What information do I need in order to make this decision?* One of the main causes of poor decision making is a lack of information. Do not make a decision before you have all the information you need to make a wise, informed decision. Take the time to learn and gather information.
4. *What are my alternatives? Which one's easiest? Which one's best?* When you are ready to move forward, it can be tempting to zero in on one option without considering all your options. Always ask yourself, *What options haven't I considered?* Also keep in mind that there are times when the easiest decision is the best decision. At other times, the best decision is the one that requires the most effort or patience.

5. *What will each alternative cost me?* Weigh all of your options and compare them. Know what the cost will be to you—and not just in terms of money, but also in terms of time, energy, relationships, space, and other resources.
6. *What other factors influence my decision?* Be honest and recognize all the factors influencing your decision. Are you making a decision because it will boost your ego or impress others? Are you in a particular career because others have pressured you? Some influences positively impact your decisions, while others move you away from the core of who you truly are.
7. *What do I feel in my spirit is right for me?* You're not alone in your decision making. Pray and listen for divine guidance. Then muster up the faith and courage to follow it.
8. *Who's the right person to help me in this?* "In the multitude of counselors, there is safety," Proverbs 11:14 (NKJV) tells us. When a decision calls for it, reach out to those who have the experience and background to help you make a wise decision. Be discreet and wise about whom you trust with helping you make a decision. Only share with those who are objective, who have proven themselves trustworthy, and who have your best interests at heart.
9. *Will this decision move me closer to my vision or pull me further from it?* When your daily decisions are aligned with your vision, you create the life you truly want. With every decision, consider your vision and make sure your decisions further it.
10. *Is the decision aligned with my values?* Identify your values. (For example, the five values that are nearest to my heart are freedom, creativity, truth, beauty, and connection.) Know what is important to you, and make sure your decisions reflect those values.

11. *What's the ideal scenario? What will it take to bring that to life?* It's often tempting to make decisions that will leave you settling for something less than God has in store. Be clear about your ideal scenario for any given situation, and reflect on whether the decision you make will help bring that ideal scenario to life. If not, perhaps it's time to either consider an alternative or wait until a better opportunity presents itself.
12. *Is the decision pleasing to God?* Ultimately, a wise decision is a godly decision. If your decision is aligned with the Word of God and God's will for your life, you can be assured it is a wise one. So be honest with yourself, and don't let your emotions guide your decisions. Do what you know in your spirit is right.

Confidence Prayer

Your Word in James promises that if I lack wisdom, I can ask You for it and You will give it to me. I am asking You for wisdom about the important decisions in my life. Show me the way. Show me Your way. Help me practice patience when it is not yet time to take action. My goal is to please You, God. Help me do what is right in Your eyes even when I am tempted to do something different. From this day forward, I pray You will grant me the confidence to make wise decisions by listening for and following Your voice.

Confidence Journal

In what area of your life are you least confident about your decisions? How will it feel to be able to trust yourself to make wise decisions in this area from this day forward? What will you have to change in order to ensure that it happens?

Confidence Builder

Today, make the choice to start being deliberate about the decisions you make. Identify a key decision that you need to make in your life right now. Then use the twelve questions above to guide you toward the right decision.

Day 26

Use Ridicule's Lessons

> I've gained tremendous confidence from rising above my circumstances and putting my faith in God more than in people.
>
> —Janice, 38

When I arrived at my new school as a fifth grader in the Five Points area of Denver, it was the first time I'd attended a truly public school—and I hated the treatment I received.

Up until this time, I'd attended parochial schools and schools on Air Force bases, and my previous schools were racially diverse (African American, European American, Puerto Rican, Filipino, and Amerasian), but socially homogeneous (all our parents were in the same line of work).

Now, due to the city's integration policies, I passed a dozen elementary schools daily as my school bus took us from Lowry Air Force Base, where we lived, to an inner-city neighborhood downtown. Only the children of enlisted people had to be bused so far; officers' kids went to school just outside the base.

From the end of fifth grade through the beginning of sixth, I endured torment at that particular school, especially from the girls. I was constantly in fights that I didn't start. I was called a variety of ugly names—rather comical ones when I think back—for "talking white," getting good grades, speaking with a southern accent, and having a big forehead. Whatever reason the kids there could come up with to harass me, it seemed they did.

To be accurate, life had been pretty good until my third day at the school. That was when, unbeknownst to me, one of the popular boys in my class said he liked me. I didn't even know who he was at the time, but apparently his statement fueled disdain from the popular girls in my class. And I was promptly told that they wanted to kick my butt. (Actually, they used much more colorful words than I'd ever even heard before, but you get the picture.)

I remember two new friends from the base delivering the message, and, naively, I wasn't even quite sure what they meant. I'd never been in a fight before, and at my last school the biggest concern among the girls was collecting Jordache purses, roller skating, and perfecting one's Atari skills.

As Dorothy told Toto, I wasn't in Kansas anymore.

There were really just a few girls who didn't like me at this new school, but unfortunately, the others followed their lead when school was in session. I didn't have problems with my friends on the base, but they kept silent when trouble started at school.

Trying to avoid the daily ridicule, I started to pretend to be sick often. I was tired of eating lunch alone and being made fun of. I was tired of not knowing if someone might punch me out of the blue in the hallway and then having to decide whether to fight back and have four more kids simultaneously jump on me.

I got into fights in the classroom, on the playground, and on the bus—and I never told my parents about any of this while it was going on. I was sure that they would show up at school in an effort to save me and end up making matters worse. So I kept silent and counted the days until our house would be built so we could move off the base and twelve miles out to the suburbs.

In total, my six months in that school felt like six years. And when I arrived in Cherry Creek School District in Aurora, Colorado, after Thanksgiving break in 1983, I felt guilty about how excited I was.

At Five Points, the majority of the students looked like me. At Cherry Creek at that time, African Americans were a very small minority (around 3 percent). I felt guilty about it, but the truth was that I was relieved to see white kids. Generally speaking, they wouldn't be angry about how I talked, critical if I excelled in school, or ready to start fights if I looked at them the wrong way. At ten years old, I was embarrassed that I felt that way, but I'd developed a real insecurity about being in a large group of black girls, an insecurity that would continue for the next five years. I was clear about and happy with who I was, but who I was didn't seem to match an unfortunate stereotype that was required to fit in at Five Points (and it's sad to see that these same issues plague young people today).

Looking back, the lesson I learned is that we can develop insecurities based on others' inaccurate and unfair perceptions of who we are or who we should be. I didn't want to be anyone other than the person God created me to be, but I wanted to be understood and accepted.

Unlike me at ten years old, you and I have choices about the environments we put ourselves in and the people with whom we associate. It's essential to put yourself around people who affirm you and accept you for who you are. If you don't, you may find yourself in constant, unnecessary doubt about your choices and decisions. If you find yourself in a situation where you can't immediately change your circumstances, stand firm in knowing that you don't have to fit in. You don't need to change in order to make others comfortable with who you are. You can be confident and content with being different from those around you.

I found this truth comforting when I wasn't accepted by people who looked like me as well as when I wasn't accepted by people who didn't like people who looked like me. The fighting words didn't end when I left Five Points. There were times in my new environment when I didn't fit in either. I couldn't join in the chatter about adventures in bleaching one's hair blond, and most of my classmates had no clue what a hair relaxer was.

In any case, at the core of all the taunts were the insecurities of those who were a thorn in my side. In an effort to make themselves feel better, certain kids had criticized the people around them who were different—and, for them, different was a threat to what made them okay and acceptable to the world around them. Because they didn't feel good about themselves, they sought to find something that would make them better than someone else.

This kind of pettiness and unkind behavior goes on in adulthood too.

Your situation may differ from mine, yet the same principle applies. Putting people down to feel good about ourselves can be disguised as something else because such childish habits don't always end when people pass childhood. It takes spiritual maturity and values to move past gossip and insecurity to a point where we don't need to put others down in order to feel important.

Every day we can see examples all around us of people who feel inferior (even though they're not) medicating their feelings by seeking to feel superior (even though they're not) to someone else. Who wants to feel they are the bottom of the ladder? No one—and many people who do will find some way to rise to a higher status by creating a rung on the ladder that is lower than their own. Of course, God doesn't see any of us as inferior to anyone else. When we truly embrace that fact, we cease the fruitless effort to heighten our status by lowering someone else's.

When you're authentically confident, you're comfortable with every person's uniqueness. You celebrate others' right to be different from you. In fact, differences don't pose a threat, but an opportunity to learn and rejoice in the amazing creativity of God. (The uniqueness of six billion people on this Earth truly *is* miraculous, isn't it? None of us think the same, look the same, or have the same genetic makeup. How can that be? It's mind-boggling, really. God is just that awesome.)

My point is this: God can grow us spiritually and teach us many lessons from the experience of being unfairly criticized, unkindly talked about, or wrongly treated. Here are just a few:

Endure Unconstructive Criticism

I once heard author and minister Paula White say, "If everybody is singing your praises, something ain't right." Even Jesus was criticized. And certainly if people found fault with Jesus, they'll find fault with you. There are times in life when there's no justification for the criticism or treatment that you receive. Whether at work or socially, there will sometimes be people in your life who pick you apart. Their goal is to make themselves feel more confident. Of course, they'll never find authentic confidence until they look within. Remember who you are and whose you are. Distinguish constructive criticism from unconstructive criticism. When you're authentically confident, you can hear people criticize or correct you without becoming insecure. You can listen and ask, "Is this true about me?" and answer honestly. If there's something you need to change, you can do so.

But when the criticism is unconstructive, its only purpose is to tear you down. The enemy's words cannot destroy you unless you give them permission. It's a valuable skill to be able to endure ridicule, criticism, and unfairness—and to see it for what it is without allowing it to define or demoralize you.

Don't Waver in Your Authenticity

In the face of unconstructive criticism, doubt will rear its head. If you're not fully grounded in God's love, purpose, and unique plan for you, you can be tempted to change who you are in order to accommodate others. I'm sure you've met people who do not seem authentic. They pretend to enjoy things they don't care about and speak in a way that pleases the "right" people but does not reflect the essence of who they are or what they really think. Authentic confidence empowers you to stand firm when the easy thing to do would be to waver. Let go of the need to be popular in exchange for satisfying the deep need we all have to be authentic in God's eyes. He loves you just as you are.

See Insecurities in Others, but Don't Allow The Insecurities to Become Your Own

One of the most tragic outcomes of our insecurities surfacing in relationship to others with insecurities is that we can become blind to entire situations. Let me explain. When others attempt to pull you down as a way of dealing with their own insecurity, and when you respond from an insecure place, you create a downward spiral that allows the other people to get away with making their insecurities your problem. And then you create a solution that is inauthentic.

For example, when I found myself in that unpleasant fifth-grade class, at times I responded by trying to fit my adversaries' mold. *Maybe if I can talk differently and act like I'm interested in everything they are interested in, they will accept me,* I reasoned. I was letting their insecurities—their fear of standing out from what the group dictated as acceptable—become my own.

But you know what? That wasn't me. I could only keep up the act for so long before there would be cracks in my fake identity. Besides, it's not fun to spend your life pretending to be someone other than who you are.

When are you tempted to allow others' insecurities to become your own? You can tell by your response to others' insecure behavior. Make the decision not to adopt others' insecurities with all the myths, misconceptions, and lies that they believe.

Don't Assume that the Behavior of Unfair People Will Be the Behavior of Everyone You Encounter

By taking others' behavior personally rather than seeing them as hurting people who hurt people, we can adopt beliefs that are unhealthy. One of the primary beliefs that stems from these experiences is the belief that you cannot trust anyone. This simply isn't true. Nowhere in the Word of God does it tell us that no one is trustworthy.

It does, however, advise us to have discernment about dealing with the people we encounter. Be wise in your interactions with others—and refuse to allow insecurities to keep you from connecting authentically and confidently. This assignment may mean setting stronger boundaries (we'll talk more about boundaries later), talking less, and listening more so that you can discern the intentions of others more quickly.

The bottom line, then, is to stand firm in who you are, making no apologies for being different. Refuse to change who you are to fit others' narrow definitions of who they think you should be, and you'll soon find reason to celebrate, not cringe because of, your differences.

Confidence Prayer

Lord, You know my past. You know the ways in which my confidence has been challenged along my life's path. Please take the words and acts that some have meant for evil, and use them for good in my life. Help me remain a trusting person driven by love and not fear. Empower me to confidently connect with others while never allowing their insecurities to become my insecurities. When I'm criticized, Lord, help me discern between the criticisms that are untrue and those that may hold some truth. Give me the confidence to face truths that may not be flattering so that I can make changes that allow me to become more of the person You created me to be.

Confidence Journal

What criticism or mistreatment in your past impacts your confidence today? In what specific ways does that past experience impact your confidence? What will you do about the past's impact on your present? Again, be specific.

Confidence Builder

Today, identify one way in which others' comments or actions threaten your ability to feel confident as you go through your day. Choose a person or people with whom you interact regularly.

For example, a family member who always asks, "Are you sure about that?" leaves you regularly second-guessing yourself. Kindly and lovingly ask the offending person to not ask you that question.

You might say, "You know, sweetheart, when I make a statement or share important information with you, you often ask me if I'm sure about it. That leaves me feeling second-guessed. Could you please not ask me that question so frequently?"

Practice confidence by having a conversation that needs to be had.

Day 27

Trust Divine Timing

> Sometimes I lose confidence when it takes longer than I expected to reach a goal. Perseverance takes a lot of confidence, but you've got to hang in there because God delivers on His promises—eventually.
>
> —SHANA, 28

After savoring the most tender filet mignon I'd ever had and breathing in an incredible view of the Pacific Ocean on that Valentine's Day in 1992, I looked across the table at the handsome, chivalrous, affectionate man who had come into my life. The look in his eyes told me something big was on his mind. I was right.

"Val, will you marry me?" Charles asked lovingly that night.

We were neighbors in Monterey, California, when we met at the mailbox one afternoon. I was in college. He was a naval officer in graduate school at the time. We became engaged, but in retrospect the timing clearly wasn't right. After ten months he moved to New York, and I moved to

Florida—and we didn't see each other for eight years. For five of those years, we didn't have so much as a phone conversation.

Then one fateful Saturday morning in 2001, my phone rang, and in an instant I recognized his familiar voice. Charles was calling simply to say, "Hello."

He was living near Washington DC, now, which was serendipitous because I had speaking engagements there and my father was on a work assignment there. Each time I visited, I saw Charles.

You can probably guess where this love story is headed.

In February 2003, eleven years after his original, heartfelt proposal, he again asked me to marry him. And now the timing was divine. We married four months later.

I've learned that so often in life, purposeful opportunities present themselves, but we must always ask, "Is this the right timing?" Even when you feel divinely inspired to do something, it's possible that God is simply planting a seed right now that He intends to bring to fruition at another time and place farther along the path of your life. If something you feel inspired to do is indeed meant to happen, it will.

Be confident in God's timing.

You don't have to know it for it to be perfect. In the course of eleven years, neither my husband nor I ever married or had children. We didn't know it, but God was growing and preparing us for each other, and He would bring us back together at the right time.

Consider the opportunities for which you need to ask, "Is this the right timing?" You can do the right thing in the wrong timing. If it is the right timing, forge ahead now! It is just as important to move forward when the time has come as it is to wait when the time has not come. If the timing is not now, embrace the opportunity to trust that God will allow all things to work together for your good in the timing that is best for you. We must surrender the need to be in control, because we're not actually in control anyway. We cannot see the big picture. But God can.

It may be in the area of a relationship or in another area entirely that you need to trust divine timing. Perhaps you are feeling pressured to do something that will stretch you too thin financially. Maybe you sense a career change on the horizon, and you are tempted to force it to happen too soon. Perhaps you are flooded with new ideas all the time and feel overwhelmed, as though you need to implement all of them all at once.

Relax. File away your inklings and go back to them when you have the space, resources, and energy. Everything doesn't have to happen now. Give your vision space to unfold over time.

Most important, be willing to follow your intuition, that divine inner compass by which the Holy Spirit can offer guidance when you listen for it. Often, God has something in store for you that is "exceedingly abundantly above all" you ever thought or imagined (Ephesians 3:20, NKJV), but you must trust Him and not try to make it happen before its time (see Proverbs 3:5–6).

As I learned from my eleven-year journey, your patience and trust will prove worth the wait. Inevitably, though, when you have to wait a long time for something, your confidence may waver. Expect that battle and resist it. Don't try to figure things out for yourself. There are some things in life that we can waste our energy trying to figure out. In those situations we must be willing to let go, pray for wisdom, and trust God.

I challenge you to identify the things in your life that you've fruitlessly tried to figure out—and then found your confidence wavering, even dwindling, with each passing day. Some of the most common topics are listed here:

- when "the one" will come into your life so you can get married
- why something happened that you wish had not happened

- how to fix someone else's problem
- when a long-awaited door will open in your life
- why some people are blessed in certain ways that others are not
- when it's taking longer than you thought to see your dream come true

Sometimes our knowledge is too limited to figure out why things happen (or don't happen) the way they do. God sees the big picture. Our job is to trust Him completely and have confidence in His ability to orchestrate opportunities. Accept what is, right now while you continually learn and grow spiritually.

When you don't know what to do or how to deal with certain situations, ask for wisdom. Stop trying to figure it out. Let go of the need to control when and how things will happen. Take a deep breath. Pray for wisdom. Then slow down and quiet down enough to hear that still, small voice whisper words of comfort, peace and wisdom into your spirit.

Confidence Prayer

Philippians 4:6 tells me, "Do not be anxious about anything, but in everything, by prayer and petition, with thanksgiving, present your requests to God." Help me relax in Your arms, God. Help me trust You more with each passing day so that my confidence will soar as I see that, with You at my side, I cannot fail. Your timing is perfect timing. Grant me more patience as I humbly seek to live within Your will and Your timing. I know that Your blessings will be worth the wait.

Confidence Journal

In what current life situations do you need to surrender control and trust God more? When will you begin to do that?

Confidence Builder

Identify what you need to stop trying to figure out and then let it go. Pray and listen for God's wisdom about how to proceed from here.

Day 28

Start Small—Now

> I believe that developing confidence is an ongoing challenge. Once you gain confidence in one area, it's time to move to the next area. I think that's why it's important to learn how to deal with the self-doubt when it comes.
>
> —Renee, 30

"Who despises the day of small things?" Zechariah 4:10 asks. I would like to remind you that just about every great opportunity begins small. Whether you are ready to lose weight, build a healthy relationship, or achieve financial independence, start small, but start now.

When legendary publishing pioneer John H. Johnson, who started his business with a five-hundred-dollar loan in the 1940s and created a five-hundred-*million* dollar empire that includes *Ebony* magazine, *Jet* magazine, and Fashion Fair Cosmetics, died in 2005, I heard a 2001 interview clip on PBS's *NewsHour.*

"If I tried to envision Johnson Publishing Company then as it is today, I simply wouldn't have tried," Mr. Johnson said. "I say to young people they should dream small dreams, because if you dream a small dream, it can become a reality."

His quote seems counterintuitive. *Dream a small dream?* Not exactly the advice I expected to hear from a business tycoon, but he made a significant point. Start small and you lay the groundwork for something big. I encourage you to dream big, but remember that big dreams come to life when we create small goals we can accomplish right now. Too often, we become overwhelmed by the vision because we never break it down into small, manageable pieces. We lose our confidence because we look at a goal that seems too large for our resources and talents right now.

The truth is, the dream may be too big for us right now! But it won't be too big when we get there as long as we have been building and growing toward the vision step by step.

That's the way you build your confidence: one step at a time.

How could you "start small, but start now"?

I love the question asked in the Old Testament book Zechariah: "Who despises the day of small things?" Gaining the confidence to go after what you want is a process. And it's this journey that by God's grace builds you into the person He created you to be. So don't despise small beginnings. That's where the fulfillment of your greatest potential begins.

I want to encourage you to simply believe in your own possibilities and stay the course as you pursue them! I'm amazed at how often we stand in awe of the accomplishments of others, as though we cannot achieve similar things. If you find yourself doing this, I encourage you to stop looking at what everyone else has accomplished and begin appreciating your own talents, experiences, abilities, and potential.

Authentic confidence means believing that character is developed in the process of getting to a particular place. Rest in knowing that God is in control, not you. Persevere because you believe—and not just in yourself (this is not motivational hype), but in a God who is all-knowing and has your best interests at heart. Remind yourself of the truth from Jeremiah 29:11: "'For I know the plans I have for you,' declares the LORD, 'plans to prosper you and not harm you, plans to give you hope and a future.'"

You can have the life you were meant to live and successfully pursue the things that matter most to you, but first you must believe that you can. You must expect success—and then take action and persevere based upon those expectations. Cultivate an attitude of positive expectancy. If a video camera had recorded your life over the past week, what would I say you were expecting? Would your actions indicate that you're expecting success? Consider these five strategies to help you overcome doubts and cultivate an attitude of positive expectancy:

- *Expect doubt and overcome it with the truth.* When you're pursuing important goals, doubts will surface. Expect them, but don't allow them to govern your actions. Make a list of your most persistent doubts and then counter them with the reasons that you can overcome those doubts. For example, if you begin to doubt your ability to be disciplined because in the past you have not stayed on track with your goals, remind yourself that this is a new day and that you are growing into a stronger, more disciplined person. Your past does not dictate your future.
- *Remember, "Nothing is impossible with God" (Luke 1:37).* When you are living within God's will for your life and fulfilling your unique purpose, you will experience divine favor. Don't become overly concerned when you cannot figure out how something will happen. Simply continue taking steps forward in faith, and God will meet you at the point of your limitation.

- *Failures and mistakes are learning tools.* Doubts and fears often grow when we fail or make mistakes. We begin to doubt our abilities. But failure today does not mean you will fail again tomorrow—not if you learn from your failure. So perhaps your relationship failed, or you failed in school or at work. I spent my entire first year of college on academic probation, yet I graduated in three years at the age of twenty and earned my master's degree a year later at twenty-one. My first-year failure was no indication of my academic or professional future. So, with every experience, ask yourself, *What did I learn from this experience that will empower me to succeed the next time around?* Then keep on pushing forward!
- *Take action every day toward your vision.* When you take consistent action toward a vision that is based on your life purpose, you begin to be aware of opportunities all along your path. But doubt can cause a vicious cycle in which you are paralyzed by fear and, as a result, never take action. When you don't take action, you also don't attract opportunities in your life. Thus, you reinforce your own doubts. Take consistent action toward reaching your goal, and you will break the cycle of fear and doubt that can keep you stuck.
- *Talk to yourself.* You read that right: talk to yourself! Proverbs 18:21 tells us, "Death and life are in the power of the tongue" (NKJV). Sometimes you simply have to practice positive self-talk. When you are feeling doubtful, tell yourself, *I can do this. It's possible! I have what it takes!* Speak positively to yourself about yourself and your circumstances, and you will discover new strength to move forward in positive ways. Sometimes you can't wait for others to encourage you. You have to encourage yourself.

Confidence Prayer

Lord, I will not despise my small beginnings. I trust that every experience, every challenge, and every success strengthens me. Thank You for building my confidence over these twenty-eight days. Please continue to build my character so that I can be a better servant for You and a better vessel of Your love. Most of all, Lord, thank You for the stability of Your Word and Your love, which together serve as the rock on which I can consistently build my confidence.

Confidence Journal

In what ways have you allowed negative experiences, mistakes, or failures from your past to dictate your possibilities for the future? Describe some specific times and places.

Confidence Builder

Now, today, start small but think big. Stretch yourself beyond your comfort zone. Use the skills you've gained over these twenty-eight days, and step up to your next level. Don't hold back. Step out—in faith and with full confidence to do all you know God is calling you to do.

In Conclusion

A New Beginning

I truly consider it a privilege to have walked with you on this journey toward confidence. And I am confident of this: our paths have crossed for a purpose—and that purpose is that you would step fully into all God has in store for you.

Although these pages are coming to an end, I invite you to come back and read them often as you continue to build even more confidence. I'd love to continue to encourage you. Visit me online at www.ValorieBurton.com, and I'll encourage you each week when you subscribe to my weekly (and free) *Rich Minds, Rich Rewards* e-newsletter.

I want you to remember how special you are in God's eyes. You've got gifts, talents, experiences, and passion that God has placed in you for a purpose. Don't minimize those things or "play small." It's time for a bigger game—time for you to step up to the plate at a higher level—and I believe you have it within you to accomplish more than you even realize right now.

As you move forward, remember there are four elements to building your confidence:

- truth
- faith
- preparation
- transformation

At the center of each of these is your faith. Faith is central to authentic confidence. As you grow spiritually, your confidence will soar. Stay connected to God day by day, moment by moment. There's no greater source of confidence than knowing that He is with you and on your side. Remember, He can do "exceedingly abundantly above all that [you] ask or think, according to the power that works in [you]" (Ephesians 3:20).

Don't limit God!

When you limit yourself, you limit the Power who is at work within you.

Acknowledgments

I feel immensely blessed to do what I love for a living and to have a supportive and fabulous publisher, WaterBrook Press. Thank you to the entire WaterBrook team for believing in my work and sharing it with the world. In particular, thank you to Steve Cobb, Ginia Hairston, Steve Reed, Leah McMahan, Joel Kneedler, Lisa Beech, William Bauers, Alice Crider, and Laura Wright.

A special thank you to Dudley Delffs for encouraging me to open my heart in this book, and to my editor, Jeanette Thomason, for your infectious enthusiasm and heartfelt encouragement.

To my husband, Charles. Thank you for supporting me, believing in me, and loving me.

To my mom, Leone Adger Murray. Thank you for being a role model of confidence for me—and for reading all of my books while they are still in the rough draft stages!

To my dad, Johnny Burton Jr. Thank you for instilling confidence in me.

To my little brother, Wade Murray. Thank you for your love and for being who you are.

Thank you to my big, loving extended family. I love and appreciate you: the Greenlees, the Burtons, the Adgers, the Bakers, the Worrells, and the Johnsons.

Angie Steele, thank you for your continued support, professionalism, and warm spirit.

Ben Laurro, thank you for always working so tirelessly on publicity for my books.

My friends at Injoy, especially Mark Cole and Brad Lomenick, thank you for opening doors that allow me to reach more people, particularly women, with a message of personal and spiritual growth. And Angie Bevilacqua, for your enthusiasm and hard work.

To you, the reader. Thank you for giving me the opportunity to serve you through my writing. This book is a manifestation of the purpose for which God created me—inspiring people to live fulfilling lives. When you read these pages, my purpose is ignited!

About the Author

VALORIE BURTON is the author of three other books that coach practical life needs: *What's Really Holding You Back? Listen to Your Life,* and *Rich Minds, Rich Rewards.* A sought-after life coach, she runs Inspire Inc., a media company that provides tools and information to inspire, teach, and empower individuals to live their best lives. She is host of *Thrive! Today,* a monthly coaching audio club in which she interviews noteworthy authors and experts, and helps women find the courage, clarity, and tools to transform their lives. She is a resident life coach and regular contributor to CBN.com, BlackAmericaWeb.com, and the syndicated radio show *Sharing Life Together,* produced by Focus on the Family. She served as the co-host of *The Potter's Touch* with T. D. Jakes and as the on-air life coach for NBC5 (KXAS-TV/Dallas–Fort Worth). Valorie and her husband live in Maryland.

Thousands of readers like you get weekly inspiration from Valorie Burton via e-mail. To subscribe to her free e-newsletter or learn more about upcoming events, teleclasses, and coaching, visit ValorieBurton.com.